THE JUNKIE PRIEST...
and the Reporter

As a newspaperman with the Hearst Headline Service in New York, John D. Harris has covered many kinds of stories. His assignments have carried him all over the U.S. and throughout Europe and the Middle East. He is accustomed to the tough and the sensitive, the good and the bad.

Journalist Harris has reported on the people and problems involved with drug addiction—more than that, he's lived it. A prize-winning series of articles in the Houston *Chronicle,* "I Lived with the Addicts," and countless other stories about the narcotics problem, have given him an unusually close look into this sickness that plagues so many unfortunate victims.

A telephone call from Father Daniel Egan one day, however, started him on an assignment that is the most dramatic story in Harris's writing career—the story of New York's "Junkie Priest."

THE JUNKIE PRIEST was originally published by Coward-McCann, Inc.

THE
JUNKIE
PRIEST

Father Daniel Egan, S.A.

by JOHN D. HARRIS

PUBLISHED BY POCKET BOOKS NEW YORK

FOR MY MOTHER AND FATHER

THE JUNKIE PRIEST:
Father Daniel Egan S.A.

Coward-McCann edition published April, 1964

A *Pocket Book* edition

1st printing..........March, 1965
10th printing.....September, 1970

This *Pocket Book* edition includes every word
contained in the original, higher-priced edition. It is printed
from brand-new plates made from completely reset, clear, easy-to-read
type. *Pocket Book* editions are published by Pocket Books, a division
of Simon & Schuster, Inc., 630 Fifth Avenue, New York, N.Y. 10020.
Trademarks registered in the United States and other countries.

L

AUTHOR'S NOTE

THIS BOOK was inspired by the story "The Junkie Priest" that I wrote for the September 1962 issue of *The Catholic Digest*.

Much thought was given to selection of the title. Some suggested it be changed to "The Junkies' Priest." Others thought it was inappropriate to associate the word "junkie" with the word "priest" in any form. In certain circles, though, Father Egan is known as "the Junkie Priest" with considerable reverence. And as this book concerns those circles it was decided, with Father Egan's wholehearted agreement, to use the present title.

The opinions on drug addiction and its related problems offered by Father Egan in this book, however, are his own and not necessarily those of his Church.

It was important that many persons remain unidentified. If any of the fictitious names I have used also happen to be the names of actual persons, this is entirely a coincidence. The locations of certain events have been changed to further obscure identities.

The incidents related are true. Re-creation of these and of conversations that took place at the time was done with the willing assistance of those who were present or who had intimate knowledge of the events in question.

I owe a special debt of gratitude to my wife, Bette, for her many hours of assistance in the preparation of this book. In addition I wish to thank Albert P. Govoni for his indispensable advice. To Elizabeth and Helen Patterson, who labored so long over the manuscript, also many thanks. My gratitude also goes to Sydney Connell of the New York City Department of Correction; Dr. Ray E. Trussell, Commissioner, New York City Department of Hospitals, and his colleague Dr. Alexander W. Kruger; Dr. Robert W. Rasor, medical officer-in-charge, U. S. Public Health Service Hospital, Lexington, Kentucky; Deputy Commissioner Walter Arm, Deputy Chief

Inspector Edward Carey and Captain Ira Bluth, all of the New York City Police Department; and George H. Gaffney, assistant to the commissioner, and District Superintendent Samuel Levine, both of the Federal Bureau of Narcotics. I owe special thanks to Sumner and Sylvia Collins for their encouragement and to Kay Sullivan, Rosemarie Ziegler and Angela O'Brien. I am also indebted to John T. Foster for permission to quote from a manuscript on hospital treatment of addicts as accepted for publication by *The Modern Hospital* and to Matthew Matlin, editor, National Council on Crime and Delinquency, for permission to quote from the booklet *Bail and the Indigent Accused*.

Many others, particularly those who have aided Father Egan's work in Greenwich Village, unwittingly contributed to the gathering of the material recorded here. To them, also many thanks.

Finally, this book could not have been written without my friends, the girls I cannot name. They willingly provided me with their own expert knowledge of addiction and other activities detailed herein. To them go my deepest thanks for their friendship and help.

JOHN D. HARRIS

New York City

FOREWORD

FATHER DANIEL EGAN and the New York City Department of Correction have, we are glad to say, an old and close relationship. Like most friendships it began informally: he walked into the House of Detention for Women one day and began to do whatever he could for many unfortunate persons detained there. To say that this kind of help is needed is an understatement; it is invaluable. And we know of few who have given themselves so selflessly and so completely in this direction as this remarkable priest. Religion, race, color or creed have played no part in his efforts, as great numbers of women imprisoned, and otherwise in trouble with the law, will readily agree.

Father Egan's astonishing activities among women drug addicts, prostitutes and thieves are, in fact, an almost ideal framework on which to illustrate some of the often overwhelming problems faced by this great city. One of these is the tragic revolving door in which so many women and girls become hopelessly trapped. Statistics show that most drug addicts become dependent on narcotics at an early age, often in their teens. They are then forced to steal or become prostitutes to maintain their habits and are frequently arrested and jailed. On being released, most have nowhere to go but back to the environment that created their addiction. And so it goes on: addiction, theft and prostitution, jail—in an interminable cycle.

More than 85 percent of the city's women prisoners are repeaters; that is, they have served time before. Many have done so incredibly often. Vagrancy and prostitution account for the largest number of our women prisoners, with theft and drug offenses also figuring highly. In a single year, more than fourteen thousand prisoners are admitted to the House of Detention for Women and the average cost of keeping one prisoner for one day exceeds nine dollars.

Thus, with our woman prison population often consisting of the same inmates time after time, it can be easily seen that vast sums in public funds are being expended without result.

For years Father Egan has been in the forefront of those who have argued, almost desperately, against this pathetically useless system. He has urged, constantly, that an answer lies in establishment of "halfway houses," or institutions where ex-prisoners can go directly after leaving jail to prepare themselves for return to normal society. His task has been—and is—unimaginably difficult, but a gleam of light can now be discerned ahead.

His principal activities have been concerned with easing the plight of that most tragic figure—the woman drug addict. In doing so he has penetrated a level of society known to few but habitués of the underworld and the most experienced police officers.

With this book a revealing light is cast into a dark corner.

We at the Department of Correction, operating a very large prison system, know well what Father Egan's work has meant to many of our inmates. He will always be welcome among us.

ANNA M. KROSS
Former Commissioner
Department of Correction
City of New York

CONTENTS

There is some soul of goodness in things evil. . . .

King Henry V, Act IV

1. THE CHALLENGE

A GIRL stepped out of the prison, her heels clicking on the stone steps. She wore a freshly pressed black suit and a neat release-day hairdo.

A man stood on the sidewalk, waiting for her. His features were lean, encompassing a firm mouth and a level gaze. The girl smiled at him. He grinned back.

They talked, their speech dropping into underworld argot.

"So, you got busted again," he said.

"I was on Forty-Seventh Street and—"

"And the trick you hustled was a cop."

"Yeah. How did you know?"

"The rollers called me the night they got you."

She shrugged.

"With an oil-burner like mine what's a girl gonna do?"

He eyed her thoughtfully. Ruby, a nineteen-year-old drug addict. A heart-shaped, dark-skinned face, hard little eyes and a forty-dollar-a-day heroin habit, a real oil-burner. A nice kid, even though he occasionally felt like hitting her with a chair.

"Where are your works?" he demanded.

"Stashed where no cop can find them."

He nodded. Soon, he figured, she would gently remove them from her hiding place. The hypodermic needle and eyedropper would come to life in her hands.

"Junk?"

"Feds cleaned out my connection before I was busted. But if I have to score I'll find a way."

She turned for a moment and looked at the House of Detention, somber in the bright morning sun. She shivered.

"I just did ninety days in that joint," she said. "Can we talk someplace else?"

They crossed the street and entered the Howard Johnson on Sixth Avenue. He ordered coffee.

1

"Ruby," he said quickly, "how long a run have you had?"
She shrugged again.

"I was turned on when I was fourteen. Stick of pot first. A fix a month later. Crazy."

"Busted how many times?"

"Four by city narcos. Once by feds."

"And now you're clean."

"Haven't had a fix in ninety days."

They both grinned at that.

"Want to stay clean?"

"Sure."

He swallowed his coffee. It was getting late; there were others to meet. He wrote the address of a small downtown hotel on a sheet of paper, wrapped it in a five-dollar bill and slapped it in Ruby's hand.

"There's your room," he said. "Call me one o'clock sharp. We'll try to get you a job and take it from there."

Ruby nodded, looking down at the table.

"Thanks," she said. "Thanks, Father."

She stared after him as he walked from the restaurant, a slight, almost jaunty figure in black suit and hat.

"That cat," she whispered, "is just too much."

She had been talking to the Junkie Priest.

Anyone, of almost any religion, might have been astonished if he had overheard their conversation. To some an inevitable conflict would seem to exist between their exchange, spoken in the jargon of the narcotics underworld, and the rolling, majestic Latin phrases, the ancient liturgy of the Mass, this priest had offered less than an hour before.

Even some of his fellow priests have never been fully able to reconcile themselves to the surface duality of his daily life.

In fact of all the people involved in the life and work of Father Daniel Egan, S.A., the person who takes his self-appointed mission with the most equanimity is Father Egan himself. In his mind, preoccupied with objectives that more often than not seem unattainable, there is no contradiction between the methods he employs to ameliorate the suffering of the addict and his life as a man of the cloth.

He does not look like a man who prowls New York's most dangerous tenements, alleys and basements. At forty-seven, gray hair tops a clear, unlined forehead; his face is pale and oddly serene. Many have been puzzled by this over the years. He seems too gentle, too fragile, to be a central figure in the weird and terrible world of the drug addict, a world he has termed a "festering jungle of pushers, prostitutes and thieves." His serenity is, in fact, due to just this. He has long become exposed to every sin of which the human animal is capable.

Those who are puzzled by Father Egan's apparent frailty often fail to note the steady eyes that can spark with wrath —as they do when an addict is mistreated—the determined cast of his jaw and the squareness of his erect shoulders. The implacable is also there, in the unwavering gaze.

Yet there is humor in him, too, a mischievous, Irish talent for baffling those who consciously or unwittingly try to thwart his purpose. He showed this shortly after his ordination in 1945, when working at a Negro mission in North Carolina. Dressed in open-necked sports shirt and slacks, he had loaded a score of Negro children on a bus for a swimming outing in the Atlantic Ocean, ninety miles away. He sat in the back of the bus with the children. The driver halted the vehicle after it had gone a few yards. He refused to move until Father Egan moved to the front section, reserved for whites. The atmosphere in the bus grew tense.

"I paid my fare," Father Egan said evenly, feeling an angry flush creep up his face. "I'll sit here." Then he leaned forward and added, slowly and dramatically, "Besides, I have colored blood in me."

Astonished, the driver tried to speak, but gave up. A few seconds later the bus rolled onto the highway. And a young voice whispered solemnly, "Father Daniel, you told a *lie*."

"No, I didn't," he reassured the child. "My blood is colored. It's red, just like yours."

He was born in New York City and retains fierce pride in his home town. Once, in a Western city, he listened with annoyance to a taxi driver's criticisms of New York and New Yorkers. Finally he startled the driver by saying, "Listen, you creep, I'm a New Yorker myself, so just drive the taxi, okay?"

His parents were Irish immigrants who raised seven sons and a daughter. His mother was a dark and beautiful woman who ran a firm but not rigorously religious home. His father was first a laborer on the New York subways and eventually a lieutenant of the New York police. Lieutenant Egan's tall and distinguished bearing was precisely suited to his vocation. He was honored by a newspaper as the city's "most popular" policeman and became known as an unofficial adviser on personal problems to men under his command, acquiring the equally unofficial title of "the Bishop."

Perhaps it was from his father, then, that Daniel Egan inherited his passionate concern for others. He is always disturbed by apathy, by animal acceptance of misfortune and suffering. There is always the urge within him to dare, to attempt, to take action. It was this restlessness, this instinctive rebellion against the human predicament, that led him to the vocation of the priesthood.

He does not remember when the idea of becoming a priest first entered his mind. Yet it might have occurred one night on a rocking, crowded subway car as he swung on a strap and felt perspiration trickle gently down his chest. He remembers studying the faces of his fellow riders. Suddenly, the monotony and resignation he saw struck him like a physical blow. He was nineteen, working on the circulation department of a Bronx newspaper, and had taken the same journey many times. But on this particular night the boredom, even hopelessness, he saw on the unsmiling features around him impelled him to vow that his own life would be different. No such fate would befall him. There would be a reason for his brief existence. He would not merely get up, go to work, go home, go to sleep, get up. . . .

His decision made, he joined a clerical students' club on Sixteenth Street, between Fifth and Sixth Avenues, as the first step to a far-off goal. One morning the club toured the monastery of the Graymoor Friars, a rambling structure perched on an 800-foot-high hill at Garrison, New York, in the Hudson River valley. He spent the day among friars in cowled habits and sandals, conscious of an atmosphere of spareness and simplicity. Even then the plight of the hungry and defeated struck a chord in him. For his emotions were stirred by the home maintained there for vagrant men, some recently released from nearby Sing Sing Prison.

The Graymoor Friars is a unique order. A red Star of David, symbol of the Jewish faith, is worn beneath the crucifix on each friar's habit; the star symbolizes the intimate relationship of the Old and New Testaments and emphasizes that Judaism was the seed that gave birth to Christianity. The order was founded by a former Protestant minister, Father Paul James Francis, a convert to Catholicism. Father Paul, as he was known, was a lifelong adherent to the teachings of St. Francis of Assisi, traditionally a fighter for human rights and a champion of victims of social injustice. In its inception, then, the order acquired a solid philosophical base for widespread activities on behalf of the destitute and humble, ranging from Texas to Japan.

When it was time to leave the monastery, Dan Egan did so reluctantly. On the bus journey back to the city he made another decision. He would become a Graymoor Friar.

Ordination came on a snowy January day in 1945, a decade after he entered the Graymoor seminary at the monastery.

In addition to mountains of classroom assignments the years had brought the exhilarating experience—for a city-raised youth—of building roads, clearing forests and quarrying rocks around the monastery. In upstate New York winters he shoveled snow and guarded truck radiators. At night, as stars glittered in dry, ringing air, he slept easily.

Later his brother Joseph came to the seminary. He too would become a Graymoor priest.

Daniel Egan's studies eventually took him to the day when, in a moving ceremony in St. Patrick's Cathedral on New York's Fifth Avenue, he became Father Daniel Egan, Society of the Atonement, a Graymoor Friar.

Whatever illusions he had entertained about the priesthood had now vanished. In their place was a dispassionate awareness of the finality and responsibilities of the life before him. For him, nothing could have been more appropriate. He now had the opportunity to do what he was meant to do—to work and live with the wretched and the desperate in slums, jails and courtrooms.

On his first assignment he lived for a year among dirt-poor Negroes in North Carolina, in the tobacco country. He immersed himself in their lives, learning tobacco farming and auctioneering—becoming part of them. It was a violent wrench when he was ordered to return to Garrison and the monastery.

Another talent had been spotted in him. He was a dynamic and eloquent public speaker. He was assigned to a group of priests with special preaching ability who traveled from parish to parish. The northeast section of the country opened up for Father Egan. He lived out of his suitcase, on trains and planes, and as he traveled, he watched and listened. When he spoke, it was in strong, clear tones. His words seemed to spring from depths of conviction. There was an intensity in him, barely hidden beneath a surface casualness. People listened to him.

Constantly he sought a foe he could confront in battle, a challenge against which he could throw his restless energy.

He had voraciously studied juvenile delinquency, and for a time he devoted himself, with furious zeal, to this problem. He preached to bobby-soxed and blue-jeaned audiences, lapsing into latest slang with astonishing facility. He strove to express theology in terms understandable to his listeners. He spoke with jolting frankness on drinking, dating and sex.

Mixing with teen-agers, Father Egan became first annoyed, then angered by the steady flow of pornography reaching them. He leafed through a few examples and threw them from him in anger. They could undo all he was trying to achieve. He decided to act. In a New England town he strode through staid, age-mellowed streets on a purposeful one-man crusade. Booksellers stared suspiciously at the priest as he extracted paper-backed obscenity from their shelves. He visited fifteen stores and returned to the church where he was staying, carrying an armful of purchases. The following day he calmly distributed them among parents assembled in the church. He informed them the material was typical of what was regularly read by their own children. A local newspaper commented somewhat nervously the next morning that his action was "believed unprecedented" in the city.

He pursued his campaign as he traveled. He purchased more obscene literature and thrust it on more astonished parents. When he heard Congressional hearings were due to begin on juvenile delinquency, he promptly mailed a choice selection to the chairman of the subcommittee conducting the hearings. The chairman was the late Senator Estes Kefauver, Democrat of Tennessee.

Father Egan was mildly surprised to receive an invitation from the senator to visit him in Washington. It was the first time his activities had stirred official reaction. But if he was surprised by the invitation he was not awed by it. Several months later, when he marched into Kefauver's office on Capitol Hill, he carried a large carton under one black-sleeved arm. After exchanging greetings with the tall Tennessean he unceremoniously dumped the carton's contents on the senator's desk. The flood of pornographic books, magazines, drawings and photographs jarred the dignity of the flag-draped room. A slight pause ensued, after which Kefauver questioned Father Egan closely on his work among teen-agers. He followed this a short time later by issuing a subpoena for Father Egan to testify before his committee when its hearings moved to New York.

Father Egan had declined to testify when merely asked; he felt that under oath he might be requested to disclose information he considered given to him in confidence. For he was already skirting the edge of the underworld. He had discovered that an alarming number of teen-agers were involved in theft, prostitution and mysterious other activities he could not yet guess at. He would not, if he could possibly avoid it, violate those confidences.

But he was not placed under oath. The senator observed that if he could not trust a priest he could not trust anybody. Father Egan discoursed for a while, then, on general problems of delinquency while the committee listened attentively. He left the hearing room with feelings of vague disquiet. The comfortable, air-conditioned quarters in which the hearing was being conducted seemed inexpressibly remote from hoodlum and switchblade-haunted streets. The hearing room was not the place to learn about those streets. The place was the streets themselves.

It was at this time that Father Egan's home base was transferred from the monastery to a newly instituted residence for friars in New York. He was assigned a room on the top floor of the five-story walk-up building at 138 Waverly Place, in Greenwich Village. Curiously, it was two blocks from where he was born.

And it was while preaching at a New York parish, a short crosstown ride from his new home, that he collided head-on with the fearsome dilemma of narcotic addiction.

2. HELEN

1

IT BEGAN without warning.

The dim interior of the church seemed empty. But a woman sat alone beside one of the white stone pillars that rose, culminating in graceful arcs, to the high ceiling.

Father Egan had been preaching a Lenten mission there for several days and had heard confessions throughout the evening. It was after 11 P.M. and he decided to say a few prayers and go to the rectory and sleep. He was close to the woman before he saw her. He paused, then approached her and spoke in a whisper. Could he help her?

She was young and attractive with slim, well-kept hands. She wore no rings and her head was closely wrapped in a black silk scarf. She looked up at him for an instant, then burst into tears and buried her face in her hands. He was not alarmed; it happened often. He sat down and spoke consolingly, urging her to be calm and to stop crying. When her sobs died she stared at him. Behind the tears he saw a neatly shaped face with wide gray eyes. She seemed to hesitate before she spoke, then blurted out her words.

"Father," she said, "I'm a drug addict."

His eyebrows rose. He peered at her closely. To his knowledge he had never met an addict. He searched his mind for what he knew about addiction. It came to little. He was, in fact, forced to admit it was confined to newspaper accounts of arrests and drug seizures and generally that drugs were detrimental to physical and mental well-being. But he was conditioned to show no surprise when informed of the most peculiar matters. He smiled reassuringly. Maybe he could *still* help her, he said.

The girl dabbed at her eyes and her tearful expression dissolved into a tight, bitter smile. She looked at him almost pityingly.

"How?" she asked. "Can you get me off drugs? I'm a nurse —I was a nurse—and I know what's wrong with me."

The tears returned and she began to cry quietly. Father Egan sighed. He asked her if she needed emergency treatment and was further puzzled when she told him she needed months of treatment. She added that the only place where that was available was at the federal hospital at Lexington, Kentucky. Yet she knew people who had been to Lexington four and five times and were still addicts. It was hopeless, she said.

In spite of his sympathy Father Egan felt skeptical. Anyway it was late and there was nothing he could do now. In as kindly a manner as he knew he told her to return in the morning at 10 A.M. when he would try to give her problem some attention. The girl shrugged and promised to come back. He watched her leave, a trimly dressed figure with her hands thrust deeply into her raincoat pockets.

In the morning there was a mission sermon to be preached at six o'clock and he rose early. He heard some confessions before Mass, gave the instruction after it, then heard more confessions. Another mission Mass was said at nine with further confessions before, during and after. It was a busy morning and he began to tire as the hours passed. As the time neared 10 A.M. he found himself looking repeatedly at his watch. Following the last confession after nine o'clock Mass he went back to the rectory for coffee.

When he returned she was sitting by the pillar in the same seat she had occupied the night before. She wore last night's raincoat and scarf but he could see her face had higher color. She was gazing curiously about the church. As he approached her she smiled in recognition. He greeted her and told her she seemed in a better mood than the night before.

"Father," she said solemnly, "you're a square."

He grunted and sat down. In the section of New York where he had been raised they practically ate squares. But he said nothing. The girl was cheerful, even if her buoyancy seemed vaguely fragile. He decided not to hurry matters; he would let her tell him what she wanted him to do. Then, if he could, he would do it. He did not have to wait long. Her mood became serious and she looked down at her lap before speaking slowly and evenly.

"Do you realize," she asked, "that I'm spending fifty dollars a day on heroin?"

His skepticism returned.

"Fifty dollars a day," he repeated. "Where d'you get that kind of money?"

"I'm a prostitute."

"Oh."

He rubbed his chin to give himself time to think. Not that what she said disturbed him. It was mild compared to some of the human behavior he encountered. He merely wanted to handle the situation as effectively as possible. He grinned at her and raised his shoulders expressively.

"All right, I'm a square," he said. "Now, how did you get into this jam?"

She sighed. There was really nothing to tell, she said.

"I was a nurse and I was dating this guy, a musician. He was very nice. How should I know he was an addict when I met him? But then he made me steal drugs from the hospital. After a while I experimented myself and became addicted too."

She hesitated and bit her lip.

"Go on," he said.

"I used to take drugs out of the patients' medications and inject them with sterile water instead. I guess it was lucky for someone the head nurse found out in time. I was fired and I lost my license. She could have had me arrested but she just told me to get out."

Father Egan listened without expression as the girl's dry and unemotional voice told him how she had tried to get a job and had failed; employers wanted references. Her musician left her. She became depressed and her craving for drugs intensified. She had sold everything she owned to raise money, her clothes, her television set, furniture, and spent it on drugs. One day she had tried to steal clothes from a department store in the hope of selling it and had been caught. The judge had released her on probation. A week later she stood before him again. This time he hadn't even looked at her as he sentenced her to sixty days.

"Since then," she said dully, "I've been to jail four other times. When I get out I pick up the first guy I can. Sometimes I get fifty, sometimes ten. I've been a prostitute for two years now. Sometimes I've hustled just for drugs. I can't think about anything but drugs, Father. I've got to stop but I can't. I've thought about getting treatment but nobody cares about a junkie, especially a junkie prostitute. I've—"

Father Egan had been listening in fascination but at these words he interrupted. What did she mean, nobody cared? If she was sick she was sick and that was all there was to it. He was surprised by the vehemence of her reply.

"That's not so, Father," she whispered fiercely. "You don't know anything about this. Addicts can't get medical treatment unless they're in jail."

He eyed her thoughtfully. She couldn't possibly be telling the truth, not in New York in 1952. And even if she was, there had to be an explanation. But he was intrigued and he had an idea. He stood up.

"We're going for a ride," he said. "I know a place that treats anybody for anything."

"Where?"

"Bellevue."

She shook her head but he grasped her arm firmly and strode with her out of the church. On Fourteenth Street he flagged a taxi. During the ride he asked her name.

"Helen."

"When did you take drugs last, Helen?"

"An hour ago. That's why I feel so good."

The taxi headed east and north and finally halted at the huge hospital's main entrance. Perhaps he was being naïve,

Father Egan thought. But his curiosity was aroused and he had to find out whether Helen was telling the truth.

To his astonishment a doctor in the hospital's admissions office convinced him she was. Addicts were not admitted merely for detoxification, to cure them physically of addiction. If they became ill, however, due to use of drugs or for other reasons, they could of course be admitted to the hospital. Many prisoners in the city's jails were sent to Bellevue's prison wards under those conditions. Some jailed addicts were, in addition, admitted to the hospital's psychiatric wards.

Father Egan listened with some annoyance, a flush creeping up his face. The doctor noticed this and shrugged.

"It's not my doing, Father," he said. "It's the procedure of the hospital."

Father Egan led Helen to the hospital's main lobby. He told her to sit down and marched to a coin telephone. He dialed three other New York hospitals and received the same answers each time. If she needed emergency treatment she should be brought in at once. If she was experiencing severe withdrawal symptoms—he noted the term—she should be brought in and they would see. Was she in convulsion? Was she in a coma? No, they were sorry but they did not admit drug addicts for simple detoxification.

He hung up and looked across the lobby at Helen. These hospitals ought to know what they're doing, he thought. He wasn't a doctor.

When he rejoined Helen he saw the color had mysteriously vanished from her face. Her eyes had become deep, luminous pools, giving her an oddly transparent, defenseless appearance. She sneezed.

"Don't worry, Father," she said in a tone so resigned that he winced. "I knew this would happen but you just couldn't believe me. Anyway, I've got to go now. I'll call you."

Before he could stop her she rose and walked quickly through the door.

2

In the following weeks the memory of Helen and the peculiar visit to the hospital rarely left his mind. It was inconceivable that she was the victim of injustice. Drug addiction could only be some kind of illness. Why was it apparently shunned in hospitals? Helen was a prostitute and of course addiction was mixed up with crime and police and so on. But that was no excuse for ignoring her condition. And how many others were in a similar plight? Almost by chance he was given the opportunity to find out.

He was assigned to preach at a women's prison. The institution was close to New York, in a New England state. He delivered his sermon to the rows of silent inmates seated before him, his words flowing in clear, ringing phrases. His effect on the assembled prisoners was not lost on prison officials. They were absorbed by the ease with which this priest made the most depressed, tense inmates relax and even laugh.

He was asked to come again. Invitations from similar jails followed and Father Egan became a familiar figure among drably dressed women behind bars.

He ached at what he saw. Each visit to each institution left him more disturbed than the last. He watched inmates in barren prison yards standing aimlessly, some slack-jawed, some screeching with laughter, and bitterly resented such denials of womanly dignity. What chance, he wondered, was there of rehabilitation in such environments? The widespread homosexuality grieved him and he was appalled to learn that so many women were serving their fourth, fifth and even sixth terms in jail. But it was their apathy that bruised him more than anything else. As time behind the walls stretched into dreary months and years many women degenerated into a dullness and stagnation that seemed tragically inimical to womanhood itself.

He made a startling discovery, one that instantly returned the image of Helen to his mind. A huge proportion of the women in each institution was made up of drug addicts, regardless of the crime for which they were imprisoned. In some jails the ratio was as high as 80 percent.

While touring one prison he observed to a silent official at his side: "It seems that the most that's being done for these people is keeping them out of sight. It's as if society considers them garbage and puts them in a can and slams the lid. Then society can't see them. But they're still there."

The addiction question nagged constantly at his mind. To learn more about it he questioned women in each jail he visited.

If you become ill on the outside, he asked, due to lack of drugs, what do you do?

Nothing, Father. Nobody helps junkies.

Can you get jobs if you want to live square?

Pretty tough. Lots of places require medical examinations. Like restaurants if you want to be a waitress. But the veins in our arms, where we've been sticking needles for years, are a giveaway. They make us self-conscious. We're scared of being turned down.

What happens then?

We go back to drugs.

How do you get the money?

We steal. We hustle.

Then?

We get busted, arrested.

And?

We come back here.

Father Egan was convinced the only way to break this circle was to aid prison inmates after they were released. He knew, of course, that the idea was not new. Sociologists and criminologists had been saying the same thing for years. But he was not conditioned by failure and he had too little experience to be disillusioned. In even his meager reading of penal literature the term "halfway house" occurred repeatedly and Father Egan's thoughts soon became polarized around this aspect of rehabilitation. His ideas were still vague. But he felt certain that the tragic inmates he encountered in prisons should at least be granted a *transitional* stage between life behind the walls and life in so-called normal society. Without this stage the change was too abrupt. It posed overwhelming problems of adjustment for the many unstable, immature, uneducated and unskilled persons held in jails. Women especially needed a brief, protective pause before venturing again into the world.

Father Egan communicated his thoughts to women convicts. They responded with cynical shrugs. The drug addicts, who needed some form of post-discharge care more desperately than anyone, were the most emphatic in their conviction that society would never take an active role in establishing halfway houses. They told Father Egan he was wasting his time.

Nothing could have been more calculated to heighten his obsession with the halfway house idea. And it was at this time that Father Egan met Lois.

He first saw her, a dark-haired, tight-lipped girl, during a prison visit. She told him she had been an aspiring actress and had modeled for fashion magazines in New York. With a hard smile she said she had once won second place in a beauty contest. She had graduated from one of California's best women's colleges and could quote at length from Shakespeare and Shelley. Her stately features were immobile as she added that she was nearing the end of a three-year sentence for prostitution.

His face framed the question: Why?

The hard smile reappeared. She explained that nothing had come of her dogged attempts at professional acting. She had run out of money and turned to prostitution. In a final gesture of hopelessness she had succumbed to heroin.

"Don't tell my mother," she said cynically.

Father Egan made Lois promise she would keep in touch with him after her release.

He was surprised to receive a letter from her a few weeks later while he was preaching in Toronto. The envelope showed the letter had been sent to him at his New York address, then forwarded. The girl had written, with apparent melodrama:

DEAR FATHER:

I don't know if this will reach you in time, but please try to help me. I cannot stand it much longer. I may not be at the above address when you return to New York, but please try to find me wherever I am. I have reached the end of my rope. I have to be out all night and it is bitterly cold. My heroin habit is now costing me $50 a day. I do not know where to turn.

Respectfully,
LOIS

He hastily replied:

DEAR LOIS:

Even if you are at the end of your rope please hang on for dear life, hang on until I get back. When I do I'll try to find you. I deeply regret being unable to tell you where to wait until then, but you and I both know the situation only too well. I wish indeed that there was somewhere in the city where you could go and feel safe and protected. Some day, though, we will have a halfway house. In the meantime, Lois, remember you can never wander so far away from God that you can't come back at the last minute. Remember your hands can never be so dirty with sin that God won't wash them clean, even at the last moment.

Always your priest friend,
FATHER EGAN

Forty-eight hours later Father Egan was back in New York, Lois uppermost in his mind. Immediately on leaving the airline terminal he boarded a subway train and twenty minutes later was knocking on Lois' door, in a seamy West Nineties building off Amsterdam Avenue. There was no answer. He questioned the building superintendent. The man shrugged. Yes, he knew Lois. She came and went. But he had not seen her for several days. No, he had no idea where she would be. He shrugged again and closed his door. Father Egan questioned neighbors and two patrolmen in a parked prowl car with the same result. Lois had vanished.

It was late when he reached the Graymoor house in Greenwich Village. On the bulletin board was a message. He read it, and dread rose within him.

FR. DANIEL—a detective from Missing Persons called. Will you please go to Bellevue Morgue to identify a body.

He borrowed a car and drove to the vast hospital on the East River. In the Missing Persons office, near the door that led down to the morgue, a plainclothesman handed him a small sheet of notepaper.

"We got this out of a dead girl's bra, Father," he said. "It's a letter from you. We found her in a basement off Amsterdam, uptown. Looks like a drug overdose. Maybe you can identify her."

Father Egan looked at the letter he had written to Lois. He nodded slowly. Yes, he said, he believed he could identify her.

After silently viewing Lois' body on the morgue slab for a few moments, Father Egan turned to go. He was stopped by a touch on his arm.

"You know, Father," the detective said, "I've been around this morgue a long time and I don't remember anything hittin' me just like this. I read that letter and I can't help feeling that if there had been something in town like that halfway house you wrote about, maybe that girl would be alive today. I hope you get it."

Father Egan stared at the detective for a moment. He thanked him and walked out. The words echoed in his ears, *maybe that girl would be alive today*. He slammed his car into gear and his mouth formed an angry, determined line. He would get it, he vowed, he would establish a halfway house in New York, if only for Lois. Somehow, somewhere, he would find a way.

Father Egan visited the great New York Public Library at Fifth Avenue and Forty-Second Street and hauled an armful of books into its hushèd reference room. Unfamiliar words stared up at him from the pages.

Opium, heroin and morphine. Codeine, dilaudid and dionin. Cocaine and marijuana. The amphetamines, barbiturates and tranquilizers.

The first use of opium seemed lost in history's mists. Notes on its effects had been found on Sumerian inscriptions seven thousand years old. The drug was included on a list of Egyptian medical remedies drawn up sixteen hundred years before the birth of Christ. Assyrians had used opium in the seventh century B.C. and it had been prescribed by Hippocrates himself. The poppy flower, source of opium, was a traditional emblem of sleep and death.

In the tenth century A.D. Arabian traders had apparently introduced opium to China. There, in continuous struggles against hardship, famine and other harsh realities, the drug's powers of fantasy were welcomed. The use of opium consequently became woven into the pattern of Oriental life.

In the backwash of colonial adventure the drug reached Europe. Early in the nineteenth century a German pharmacist succeeded in isolating morphine from its opium base. And by meaningful and convenient coincidence the hypodermic needle was invented at about the same time. The combination provided an unprecedentedly swift and efficient pain-killer.

In the American Civil War morphine injections were administered liberally and almost indiscriminately to wounded servicemen. Only then were the addictive powers of morphine fully realized; so many soldiers became addicted that their condition became known as "the Army disease."

Thousands of Chinese laborers, imported to build the railroads to the West, brought an opium-smoking habit with them. Many Americans, working at their sides, also acquired the habit. Meanwhile, opium and opiates continued to be marketed without restriction throughout the country. Many years were to pass before this was curbed by federal legislation.

The year 1900 marked a particularly important event in humanity's long relationship with narcotic drugs. German chemists developed a new drug that they called diacetylmorphine. They presented it for sale as a safe substitute for its parent—morphine—and even as a cure for morphine addiction. The drug was a crystalline powder, variously snowy white, gray or brown. It was marketed under a shorter name: heroin.

The new drug was welcomed by doctors until another and

alarming discovery was made. Heroin was viciously addictive itself, five times more so than morphine.

Drug users, though, especially opium and morphine addicts, were generally enthusiastic about heroin. The mere sniffing of a few grains produced faster, stronger effects than repeated pipes of opium or injections of morphine. Heroin produced unprecedented, intense and unbearably pleasurable reactions of exhilaration and drowsy content, so much so that it swiftly became the drug addict's overwhelming narcotic choice. The underworld, too, welcomed the advent of heroin, but for different reasons. The drug's extreme potency meant that immensely valuable quantities could be concealed and transported in small packages.

The resultant social problem was shattering.

In New York City, where half the nation's estimated sixty thousand drug addicts were concentrated, heroin users obtained almost seven hundred thousand dollars each day through theft, prostitution, forgery and other crimes. Individual addicts sometimes spent one hundred dollars a day on the drug, creating a never-subsiding avalanche of crime.

Seeking more information, Father Egan rode the subway downtown to the offices of the New York City Police Department Narcotics Bureau and the Federal Bureau of Narcotics. At both he was received courteously but warily; officials were curious about his impassioned interest in the subject. They pointed out that while they were indeed sympathetic with the plight of the addict, they were charged with enforcement of narcotic laws. They were not, it was regretted, social welfare agencies.

Father Egan decided he was faced with a direct challenge. It was insanity to jail addicts and then release them into the same environment that had created their addiction. There they almost automatically became readdicted and were thus eventually jailed again. The system was a brutal, medieval treadmill. He felt he had been ignorant of this callousness for too long. It was a problem he could no longer ignore; it was decidedly his business. He remembered, with bitter self-reproach, how he had asked Helen to return to the church the following morning. Why had he not at least tried to help her that night instead of permitting her to walk alone into the streets? He resolved never to repeat this error. In fact he would do more. He would seek out those who might need his help. And he felt he would not have far to go to find them.

Two blocks from his home stood a gaunt city jail, the House of Detention for Women.

3. THE PRISON

1

THE STREETS of Greenwich Village are colorful and informal, lined with art stores, secondhand bookshops and sidewalk restaurants. But in the neighborhood's center, at the busy intersection of Sixth Avenue and Eighth Street, the House of Detention for Women looms up for twelve gloomy stories of reddish-brown stone. The building is bleak and fortresslike, with rows of identical barred windows studding its formidable walls.

Leisurely strollers crowd the Village streets on warm evenings. Sometimes, when near the prison, they hear loud and occasionally obscene exchanges between youths on the sidewalks and women locked in the cells above.

The House is the only women's institution of the New York City Department of Correction, operating a system of jails and prison wards housing almost ten thousand persons. For many years the department has been urging that the House be closed and its inmates transferred to quarters less crowded, less confining, providing more light and air.

The prison's boxlike cells, measuring five by eight feet, were designed for one prisoner each. Yet they are invariably occupied by two, with cots placed little more than inches apart. The entire institution was designed to house four hundred and sixty-one inmates but is sometimes occupied by two hundred more. The oppressive overcrowding frequently raises prison tensions to hysteria level and one sobbing woman can provoke screams and tears in hundreds more. When this occurs the din echoes eerily through twelve floors of steel and stone, often unnerving the most hardened prison guards. On a spring night in 1958 the House virtually exploded when two teen-aged prisoners attacked their guards, sending scores of other inmates into rioting pandemonium. A crowd of more than a thousand gathered on sidewalks outside and listened in uneasy fascination to animal-like howls as crockery and burning bedsheets were hurled from the cell windows.

But life in the House mostly passes in uneventful, dreary monotony. Guards switch on the lights at 6:30 A.M. and the day begins with hundreds of women and girls yawning, singing and squabbling. Those with cell windows overlooking the streets often stare silently for a few minutes at early Village traffic below. For those whose cells face Greenwich Avenue the scent of freshly cooked doughnuts rises, with unbearable sweetness, from a bakery opposite the prison. In the confined quarters—each cell contains a sink, table and clothes locker in addition to the two cots—they dress and comb their hair, then troop to breakfast, usually hot or cold cereal, powdered milk, jelly and dried fruit. Following breakfast they are locked in their cells while guards change shifts. By 8 A.M. each inmate is expected to be at work or in a classroom.

In this routine their days, months and even years are spent in a hazy confusion of kitchen duties, laundry and linen room details, in sewing class, knitting class, typing class, cooking class.

In the prison's beauty parlor girls fuss over inmates due for release the following day. When a girl is leaving she is followed down the elevator by cries of "Good luck, honey! Don't look back! You'll make it okay!" On reaching the sidewalk outside she sometimes turns and waves for a moment at the rows of windows above her, at the girls still waving goodbye.

As a concession to femininity, some bars inside the jail are painted in pleasing pastel shades of pink, blue and peach. Scattered among the inmates are determined Lesbians, and the House often provides a damaging experience for teenagers jailed for the first time. Women are imprisoned there for almost as wide a range of offenses as committed by men:

in addition to prostitution, they are held for abandonment, abortion and arson, forgery, fraud and gambling, murder, kidnaping and drunken driving, perjury, resisting arrest and inciting to riot, assault, both felonious and simple, and many more.

Problems associated with imprisonment of very young women have on occasion aroused special concern. On August 10, 1961, *The New York Times* commented:

> The approach in New York City and State to the problem of wayward adolescent girls aged 16 to 21 years, who are in deep trouble with the law, is a disgrace.
>
> Unlike most delinquent boys whose acts are illegal, the girls are mostly immoral. Most girls get picked up for promiscuity; many succumbed to drugs and will solicit or resort to crime to appease their sick minds and bodies; others are young alcoholics; others have pregnancies out of wedlock. The city's Commissioner of Correction, Anna Kross, has long pleaded for recognition that these girls need medical and psychiatric care, not the lock-up.
>
> Yet in this city most are thrown in the House of Detention for Women. This is a fortress of despair—an overcrowded, maximum-security prison, whose heavily barred cells house young offenders and habitual criminals alike.

Other newspapers in the city have referred to the House as an "island of misery," a "school where daily lessons are given in crime, drug addiction and sexual abnormality," and a "woman trap." A woman reporter who toured the building wrote:

> Inmates under twenty-one are segregated, as are the narcotics addicts. The "tank," three bare cells with sliding peep-holes in the steel doors, is used only for the occasional addict whose cries during withdrawal disturb the other inmates. . . .

A Canadian prison chaplain visited the House. His verdict: "It should be bombed."

Correction Commissioner Anna M. Kross, a former city magistrate, has herself referred to the House as "barbaric," "degrading," "indecent" and a "hell hole." One newspaper quoted her, as early as 1955: "Why they ever built this Alcatraz I'll never know." From the date of her appointment as Commissioner in 1954, Mrs. Kross has tried to institute reforms. But, as a departmental report tersely noted, "Inadequacies of appropriated funds and existing facilities have kept the city's prison system from doing more." The same report observed:

> The basic goal of penology is to change the anti-social attitudes of inmates while institutionalized. The real test of correctional success comes, however, when the inmate is released back to his own community. It is at this point that he is apt to relapse into his anti-social behavior. Penological studies show the very obvious advantage of after-care of released inmates. Such facilities as clinics, parole and guidance counseling are invaluable to the released inmate in enabling him to maintain the changes that have taken place. Therefore, we urge the establishment of a new unit for the after-care of released inmates, especially narcotic addicts, to provide these services.

The House is everything it has ever been called. But for some women it is also the only home they have ever known. It is a club to which they return repeatedly to meet old friends. No physical ill-treatment, no beatings, occur there. The institution itself batters its inmates. But in further paradox, for many inmates the House is the one place they know in their lives where they eat adequately and regularly and where they are provided with shelter and medical care.

"A girl might come in here looking like she's in the last stage of terminal cancer," a House employee observed. "If she's on drugs, it's a sure bet she hasn't been eating. After a few weeks here you wouldn't recognize her. She's put on weight, we may have given her glasses and fixed up her teeth. If she's like most girls, she will have adjusted to prison life quickly. It's a prison, it's not a sorority house, yet it's got a kind of mothering quality. We put her to bed, we wake her up, we feed her and we clothe her. If she's sick we take her to the doctor, if she's bad we punish her, if she's good we reward her. Just like mother. I've had girls call me and tell me how sorry they are to be on the outside. Their whole personalities change when they're in here. By and large, on the outside, they're chaotic and unproductive. Yet in here they become almost compulsively organized. Women who never knit become great knitters. Women who never read find they read two, three, four books a week in here. They're conscientious in their work assignments. They keep their cells beautifully clean and neat. Mostly they're friendly, kind and warm to each other. As far as jail depression goes, most of the so-called anxiety symptoms begin to show a few days before they're due for release. In fact it's interesting to note that our psychiatrist will often begin to prescribe tranquilizers to inmates just before they leave, not when they arrive. And the reason is simple.

"When a girl goes out of here, she's entitled to twenty-five cents and a baloney sandwich. I don't remember in seven or eight years anyone taking that sandwich. It's horrible. Sometimes a girl will get a few dollars extra from volunteer groups who work here. But with the kind of turnover we have, it's usually a lot less than ten dollars. Mostly, though, she just gets the twenty-five cents.

"Now this is the crucial moment. When the average girl walks out of here she doesn't know whether to turn left, turn right, or walk across the street. Now I'm talking about the first ten or twenty seconds after she's released. She's got no plans, no family, nobody. No one will hire her. We can't do anything for her. And after she's had the security—and I really mean security—that this place offers, this can be a very disturbing experience. As a result, she's often back in a few days or weeks, depending how quickly she's caught either shoplifting or prostituting."

2

It was into this world, moonlike in its remoteness from the city that encompassed it, that Father Egan came when he first sought to give aid to drug addicts. Almost immediately he was recognized by former acquaintances and shouts echoed through the jail.

"Hey, Father! Ain't you the one who came to see us upstate? What the hell—sorry—what're you doin' in this dump?"

And: "Say, you're the priest I met in the Jersey joint last year. You told me to look you up if I hit New York. But you beat me to it."

He discovered that working among convict women came naturally to him. He felt at home among steel bars and prison corridors. He quickly found there was much to be done and was soon trying to find jobs, clothing and occasionally lawyers for girls when they were released.

In return the girls confided in him, guardedly at first, then openly, finally holding nothing back.

"I was a hundred-dollar call girl once, Father," a woman related wistfully. "I had a poodle on a leash, a high-class apartment and a high-class clientele. I used to walk on Central Park South and stop traffic, I looked so good. I had nothin' but class, an' look at me now."

He looked, and saw an aging, ravaged addict.

One girl made him especially thoughtful. She was young and her oval face was childishly serious as she tried to explain her addiction.

"It's like this, Father," she said earnestly, as they sat together on a bench in a House waiting room. "I've been hustling for five years now and I'm only twenty-two. But I still have my conscience and my self-respect. I'm not like *some* of these tramps in here. Because for me the only way I can continue is to take drugs first. They deaden my conscience."

"So why hustle?" he asked.

She lifted her thin shoulders.

"I just never been able to make it any other way," she replied despondently. "I was never able to learn nothin' and I could never hold a job more than a day. Maybe there's something wrong with me. But I still got to eat."

He eyed her warily. Was he being conned, by an expert? Yet perhaps she was telling the truth. So he chalked it up as a lesson learned: There were girls who could not find or hold jobs and thus became prostitutes; they took drugs to become insensitive to shame; they became addicted and were forced to prostitute themselves to obtain money for drugs. . . .

He scratched obediently in his notebook as the girl asked him to write to her mother, to square things with her father, to visit her baby at a foundling home.

Occasionally he stood in the ground-floor corridor and looked into the House rotunda, a circular hallway near the prison's exit. On one side of the hallway was the door to Greenwich Village and the world. On the other, slim steel bars glinted to the ceiling, separating the rotunda from the prison corridor. In their center was a barred door, guarded day and night by a male, uniformed Department of Correction officer.

Shortly after Father Egan began to visit the jail a woman pounded late one night on the street door from outside, begging to be allowed *in*. Once inside she crumpled to her knees, then rolled across the floor like a rag doll. She was in an extreme, dangerous stage of heroin withdrawal, in agony from her scalp to the soles of her feet. She pleaded hoarsely for relief, insisting that she did not know of anywhere else to ask for help. Prison guards tried desperately, by telephone, to get a hospital ambulance to come for her. Finally they called Father Egan. He arrived ten minutes later.

He glanced at the woman and furiously dialed a city hospital. "Now listen," he said. "We've got a sick woman here. She's a drug addict. But she's also an emergency case. Somebody had better pick her up."

He was adamant about the severity of the woman's condition and finally an ambulance was dispatched. It marked the first time he had obtained a hospital admission for an addict. Now, he felt, if he were to be as insistent in the future as he had been in this case, he would secure the admissions of many more.

Soon he began to receive letters, a flow of pencil-scrawled messages on cheap, lined notepaper that was to become a continuous flood over the years. The letters were sent down from the cells in such numbers that the prison administration finally provided him with his own mailbox. This was a brown manila envelope with his name on it, scotch-taped to a first-floor corridor wall.

DEAR FATHER EGAN,

May I see you right away. I am very depressed. I am doing three years. I have been here 9 months.

Thank you,
KATY DUGAN
11th floor dorm.

FATHER EGAN,

Would you please see me at your convenience. I am pregnant and I have problems I must discuss.

Thank you ever so much,
C. LYNN
11th floor dorm.

FATHER EGAN,

May I please see you today. I was sentenced to 2 yrs. for theft. I am very bitter because I feel I was sentenced wrong. Without a lawyer, aid or anything. I just left from doing four months and I was out four weeks. Why did I go back to drugs and prost? Because when I left here I had no money nor anything. And these people put me in the streets like an animal. So with nowhere to go and no one to turn to I had to go back to my old friends and what have you. I am about to have a baby any day and I want to be able to take care of my son or daughter. This might be a good thing for me. Please help me.

ETHEL COOLEY
11th floor dorm.

FATHER EGAN,

I was hoping when you came today you might be able to see me. I'm going home next Tuesday or rather I should say I'm going into the street. For I have no place to live. My mother always used to help me when I got out but she is finished with me this time. I would like to prove to myself I can make it without junk or hustling.

But how can I without a roof over my head? If you can help me or have any suggestions, please call me today. Thanking you in advance.

Sincerely,
GRACE OWEN
5th floor.

He read them, offered a prayer and tried to solve each girl's problem.

But if there was sadness inside the House, outside there was pure horror.

4. THE JUNGLE

1

IN THE narcotics underworld of New York Father Egan found a nightmare. He entered a grotesque, terrifyingly illogical society where the half-starved and homeless spent one hundred dollars a day on drugs, where prostitution, forgery and theft were normal pursuits and where sickness was mystifyingly a crime.

He was, however, swiftly accepted into this weird and suspicious fellowship. Girls released from the prison told of a priest who, far from being repelled by their activities, was striving to understand them, who would extend any possible aid and whose confidence could be implicitly trusted. These were impressive credentials and the news spread rapidly wherever addicts gathered.

Now Father Egan began to receive strange calls at odd hours providing him with whispered information or asking for immediate help. Many of the pleas came from women who had sought his help while in the House. Through them the curtain was ripped aside on the utter wretchedness of the addict's condition.

He stepped from the prison one day with a rigidly tense

woman. Her eyes, deep in her sallow, high-cheekboned face, blinked nervously in the morning sunlight. They were eyes that reflected fifteen years of addiction and jail.

"Father," she said suddenly, "I'm through, and that's a promise. I'm tired. I'm thirty-three years old and I've had it. I can't do any more time. It'll kill me if I have to come back here. I'm going home to mother and I'll never use drugs again."

He listened thoughtfully. She spoke with an air of quiet finality.

"Good, Hilda," he said cautiously. "I've been waiting to hear you say that."

He found her a job in a laundry. The job paid sixty dollars a week, which he knew was less than Hilda could earn in one night. But she was grateful and clasped his hand. Her mother wept and thanked him.

On the third day Hilda failed to show up for work.

Her mother called him, fearful. She had not seen her daughter for twenty-four hours. He tried to reassure her, but a sense of impending tragedy was evident in his voice. Three days later Hilda called him. Her voice sounded like a phonograph record played at too slow a speed.

"Father, I'm a problem," she croaked laboriously. "I'm a mess. I slipped again. But I'm trying to kick, honest I am. You got to believe me. Mama's locked me in the room an' I'm doing it cold turkey. Please come an' see me. . . ."

"Sure, Hilda. Stay right there. Don't leave the room."

Hilda lay on her bed, crumpled under a heap of soiled blankets. Her mother, face sagging with despair, sat by her side. As he approached the bed Hilda screamed, then screamed again. She rolled off the bed and hit the floor heavily, hands clutching her stomach, eyes rolling wildly.

"Out," she whispered hoarsely, "I'm goin' out. I'm not gonna do any more of this. It ain't worth it."

Father Egan threw his coat on a chair.

"Don't go out, the narco cops are on the street," he lied to her. "You've got to stay in here. Everyone in the neighborhood's laying low. No one's going to score around here today."

With her mother's help Father Egan tried to lift the shuddering woman back to the bed. But she groaned like a wounded animal and squirmed away, her body twitching and retching beneath her robe. She rolled under the bed and thudded her head against the wall. Together they pulled her out and forced her back on the bed.

He looked about the tiny apartment and met the mother's shamed eyes. The stench was terrible.

"I know, Father." She wept. "I make her coffee an' she brings it up. She can't even make it to the bathroom."

Hilda was in her third day of withdrawal and gradually, as dusk filled the room, her misery dwindled to shivering perspiration. She had been fighting for seventy hours and was totally exhausted. Panting, she gazed at Father Egan.

When the room was dark he picked up his coat and told Hilda's mother he would return the following day. "Call me any time," he added. "Day or night."

The call came three hours later. The mother's voice was sad and resigned.

"Hilda busted out of here an hour after you left, Father," she said quietly. "She came back like a lamb in fifteen minutes. She got a shot before she hit the end of the block. Now she's peaceful, sittin' here watchin' television."

And after all that, he sighed. After all that.

But he was never discouraged by failure. It merely drove him to greater determination. He was in a battle and he would fight, if it took all the courage and will at his command. He found he was in constant need of these qualities, as on the night an anonymous caller told him that Corinne, a reedlike addict he had known in the jail, was being forcibly held as a prostitute in a Brooklyn apartment.

"These guys are keepin' her high on dope, Father," the caller confided. "A little, mousy kid like that. She don't know what's happenin' to her. But I heard about you an' I thought I'd give you a call. So listen—the gorilla who's keepin' her is gonna be out of the apartment for a couple of hours tonight. He's got the kid so scared and dizzy she won't step out the door alone. He's leavin' pretty soon an' I think someone could get her outa there if he moved fast. But no cops— okay?"

"No cops," Father Egan replied quietly. "Just give me the address."

The drive from Greenwich Village to the far end of the Brooklyn Bridge seemed impossibly long. But eventually he parked outside a gray apartment building. The street was deserted and scraps of paper tumbled on the sidewalks, driven by a wind from the nearby East River. He turned into the doorway and began to mount a narrow staircase.

A man appeared at the head of the stairs. For an instant his gaze locked with that of the priest. Father Egan immediately recognized him from a picture he had once seen in Corinne's purse. The man was huge, with a broad, fleshy face, a cigar clenched in his teeth and small eyes under a low forehead and close, matted hair. He wore a drab windbreaker and heavy work pants. He seemed startled at the sight of the black-clad figure climbing toward him. He descended the stairs slowly and looked warily at Father Egan as he passed him. Father Egan nodded, then caught his breath as he heard the footsteps halt behind him. He felt the small eyes boring into his back.

He reached the second floor. Corinne's apartment was to his right, its door inches from his hand. Without pausing he climbed the next flight of stairs and knocked at the nearest door. A woman answered, also surprised to see a priest.

"Is this Mr. Moran's apartment?" Father Egan inquired smoothly.

"No, it ain't, Father. You got the wrong address. Something's wrong, huh?"

As she spoke, he heard the hoodlum continue down the stairs, apparently satisfied. The street door slammed.

"No, I'm sorry to have troubled you," he replied. "God bless you."

He ran down the flight of stairs and pounded on Corinne's door. It opened and he pushed his way in. The girl looked at him dreamily, pushing back her hair and swaying slightly. Her small white face was discolored by a massive bruise beneath her left eye. Without speaking he led her gently from the apartment. She followed him unprotestingly and when they were seated in his car she asked, with mild curiosity, "Where we goin', Father?"

"Bellevue."

During most of the ride to the hospital he was silent. He finally asked Corinne to give him her captor's name and telephone number. After she was admitted to Bellevue, for treatment of shock and bruises, he dialed the number she had given him. On hearing the suspicious grunt, he coldly explained he was the priest on the stairway and that he now had Corinne in his care. His voice hardened. "And if you so much as talk to her again I'll personally make it my business to see every cop in the city starts looking for you."

He hung up, his face grim, wondering what effect such brutality had on a girl like Corinne. A week later he found out. On her release from hospital she had deliberately solicited a detective in order to be imprisoned again in the House of Detention. When he confronted her, she shrugged.

"It's safer in here, Father," she said. "I'll rest awhile."

But at least she appeared well-fed and relaxed after her week in Bellevue, and that was something.

On another night, with gale-force winds battering the streets, he drove from hospital to hospital with an eight-months-pregnant prostitute-addict, her head slumped in the misery of withdrawal. At each stop she was refused admittance; her withdrawal symptoms were not considered severe enough for hospitalization. As for her pregnancy, he was told there were two or three weeks to go before she would need medical care.

"What about the unborn child?" Father Egan demanded. "You know the baby could be *born* addicted. Have you ever *seen* a child born that way?"

Anyone who had seen it could hardly forget it. Addicted mothers often give birth to children with all the symptoms of acute withdrawal: tremors, pallor, piteous cries, yawning, sneezing, sensitivity to touch, vomiting and diarrhea. Phenobarbitol, paregoric and tranquilizers are administered, sometimes for five or six weeks after birth, until a cure is effected. But no one seems to know what permanent damage, if any, is suffered by the infant.

A week later the girl was admitted to a hospital. She was carried in, semiconscious with pneumonia. Her baby was born dead. Father Egan listened impassively to an emergency room nurse's remark that she had never seen a pregnant woman in so advanced a stage of malnutrition.

The months dragged into a year and the nightmare continued. An unknown community of homeless and desperate women existed in the city, some of them sleeping in empty trucks and hallways. And although he was becoming conditioned to the most hideous of human experiences, he was occasionally stunned by single, agonizing barbs.

One afternoon, on a crowded Village street, he came face to face with a woman he had last seen in the jail several months before.

"Hi," he greeted her.

"Well, if it ain't Father Egan." She smiled.

Automatically she proffered her hand and, as Father Egan grasped it firmly, she tensed. He felt a strangeness in her grip and released the hand. He looked down and was shocked to see three fingers were missing. His eyes framed the question: *What happened?* The smile vanished from the woman's face and tears came to her eyes.

"Father, you got to forgive me, please," she whispered. "But I jus' didn't want any more needle marks on my arms. All the veins had collapsed. I started usin' the needle between my fingers an' my hand got infected. They had to amputate. . . ."

The sight of the mutilated hand remained in his mind for days.

It was no worse, though, than his telephone ringing at 4 A.M. a week later and a girl's voice asking him, calmly, "Father, can you come an' get me? I'm by the river off Canal Street. Some guys were gonna throw me in, but they've gone now."

She gave him the location: a coin telephone by a Hudson River pier. He dressed hurriedly and drove through a deserted wilderness of factories, warehouses and parked trailertrucks, graying in early light. He found her, an unsmiling teen-ager with weary eyes, shivering in the chill morning air. During the drive uptown to her home she explained what had happened. He listened incredulously.

"Well, Father," she said, "I was up there in the Bronx in this guy's place an' I took a shot an' got sick. I don't know what was in that stuff but I almost passed out. I was throwin' up and everything. There were a few guys there an' I begged them to take me to the hospital. I felt like I was dyin'. So these creeps go into a huddle while I'm lyin' there. They're all pushin' junk like crazy, big operators, an' they were scared I'd squeal on 'em if I went to the hospital. As if I'd do anything like that.

"So, anyway, they get into an argument, screamin' at each other, about what to do with me. Next thing I know someone's grabbing my arm an' I feel another needle goin' in. I tried to fight this guy off 'cause I halfway know what he's doin'. He was givin' me a hotshot."

Father Egan eyed her quickly. Her neat profile was composed. A hotshot was an injection of heroin poisoned with cyanide. Its purpose: to kill the user.

"But the hotshot wasn't hot enough," she continued complacently. "I jus' felt worse than I was feelin' already. Only these jerks were too dumb to see that. They load me in a car an' throw me on the floor an' start drivin' around town still hollerin' to each other. Finally, one of 'em yells, 'The river!' An' they all join in yellin', 'The river! The river!' An' I'm lyin' there listenin' to all this with their feet on me. Next thing I know the car stops an' they shove me out. Only when I hit the ground and sniffed the air a couple of times I came alive an' sat up. So they all let out a howl an' leave. An' there I am sittin' on a pier, all alone."

She shrugged, adding laconically, "I had a dime, an' you're the only one I know in this miserable town who'd get me out of a jam. So I called you."

She lit a cigarette and settled back comfortably on the car seat, allowing the air to whip through her yellow hair. Father Egan observed her from the corner of his eye and shook his head. He drove steadily north on the West Side Highway, the river dark and gleaming to his left, a strip of white sky visible between midtown skyscrapers to his right.

"How are you feeling now?" he asked.

"Okay. Sleepy, I guess. A little scared."

There were few cars on the highway at the dawn hour and he drove swiftly and easily to the street where she lived. He remembered a similar journey a few days earlier, when he had weaved desperately through jammed midday traffic on the same highway, his palms sweating, his throat dry.

A call had come as he was about to eat lunch.

"I can't stand it, Father," the young voice stated flatly. "I got to get out of here and take a fix. There's nothing I can do about it. I've been tryin' to fight it, but I know when I'm licked. I hate to ask you to do this, but I don't know nobody else to ask. Can you come here right now and baby-sit for me until I get back?"

"Baby-sit? Well, Josie, I . . ."

"Father, I love my baby, but I got no time to talk about it. I got to go, *now*."

The telephone went dead in his hand.

Twenty minutes later, after a wild drive from the Village, he walked into Josie's apartment. Something moved in an open kitchen drawer. It was Josie's three-month-old son, snug and clean in a blanket. The baby stared up at him, blue eyes solemn. He relaxed and picked the child up in his arms. He looked for a moment about the one-room slum and saw a coverless mattress, a rusting stove, a chipped refrigerator, the cabinet, peeling walls and a single cracked window. No baby carriage.

He drove slowly downtown to the foundling home, one hand on the wheel, one hand on the baby.

2

At first his reasons for devoting himself to female addicts instead of addicts in general were uncomplicated and practical. The first addict he had met had been a woman and mission work had taken him into women's prisons. Both had carved indelible impressions on his mind. And when so many of the girls he had known in those prisons came to New York, again to prison, he felt there was enough for him to do without seeking similar problems on Riker's Island, Hart's Island, the Tombs or the other male prisons in the New York area.

Other factors soon emerged. The deeper his involvement in female addiction became the more he was convinced that a special need existed for coping with this particular aspect of the over-all addiction problem. For whatever difficulties the male addict faced in his terrible dilemma they were minor in comparison to those faced by women. Female addicts were shunned by society as hopeless, as its untouchables, as the scrapings of its barrel. Any addict was branded with the stigma of the underworld but the factor of prostitution further outraged society. The prostitute-addict was too squalid for society's awareness, let alone its sympathy. And if she was a Negro, society's recoil often teamed with racial prejudice to cast her completely into the darkness.

They were the easiest prey for the sadist, the sex criminal and the brutal pimp. They were, in fact, defenseless before the savagery of their own lives. And each time Father Egan found a woman who had been beaten, each time he saw a woman weep through blackened eyes, each time he found a woman unconscious in a hallway, his devotion to all of them grew.

More ramifications of the problem became evident. The illicit aura surrounding addiction cast a morbidly fascinating glow and the subject provided obvious material for sensational journalism, both printed and broadcast. Addicts, like welfare recipients, were easy to crusade against; there was little fear of anyone of influence or stature responding on their behalf. Their leper status frequently made them targets of unnecessarily harsh police action and often resulted in hurried, superficial courtroom procedures. A sick, ragged junkie presents an unpleasant, objectionable sight in a courtroom.

One of the immediate tasks Father Egan faced was an attack on the popular image of the addict as a "dope fiend," as a slavering maniac freed from fear and inhibition by drugs and seeking to plunge himself and his victims in an orgy of murder, rape, robbery, perversion and sadism. The truth is that opiates, since their earliest use, have been instruments of self-induced torpor and relaxation. Heroin in particular depresses the libido and inhibits sexual desire. Many homosexuals use the drug for this reason; it diminishes their sexual drive and helps lessen their conflict with society. Sated with heroin, an addict becomes passive and dreamy. He can be desperate and dangerous in efforts to obtain the drug, but once under its influence becomes indolent. Heroin renders him, in the argot of addiction, "on the nod."

3

On a visit to Washington, D.C., Father Egan dialed the headquarters of the Federal Bureau of Narcotics. He asked for Commissioner Harry J. Anslinger and was surprised to learn the commissioner was anxious to see him.

Father Egan walked briskly into the drab United States Coast Guard building on Pennsylvania Avenue, home of the bureau, and was directed to a corner office on an upper floor. Anslinger rose from behind a large desk and came forward to greet him.

Father Egan eyed the commissioner with interest. He saw a heavily built, round-faced man with bland eyes and a wide smile. Anslinger was a controversial figure, a champion of those who favored a rigid, law-enforcement approach to the narcotics problem. But Father Egan was determined to keep an open mind. The commissioner had twenty years of experience in the narcotics field; he was a high federal official who spent four million dollars a year and controlled an agency of some four hundred employees. His agents were active throughout the country and the world and their reports were channeled to this desk.

Anslinger, in turn, seemed surprised and pleased to see him. He informed Father Egan he was well aware of his activities and added that he was the first priest to have visited him during his years in office, years when he had worked under constant criticism from people who, he said, knew little about the problem. Launching into vigorous defense of his policies, Commissioner Anslinger noted that federal statutes had to be enforced and that he was empowered and equipped to enforce them. It was dirty, dangerous work often performed among unspeakable, ruthless elements of the American and foreign underworlds. As for narcotics racketeers, non-addicts who trafficked in drugs, the commissioner felt they deserved only the harshest of punishment. He also appeared convinced that most addicts had criminal backgrounds before resorting to drugs. This brought a puzzled frown to Father Egan's face. The addict had to be removed from society, the commissioner continued, whether by imprisonment or hospitalization. Yet he stressed the necessity for compassionate treatment of the addict and for his rehabilitation into normal society.

The commissioner concluded the meeting by autographing a book on narcotics for Father Egan. As the priest was about to leave, Anslinger stopped him.

"One thing more, Father. Any time you have an addict who you feel needs my help to get her into a hospital, call me collect. There's never been an addict who's asked me for help for whom I haven't been able to do something."

Silently Father Egan told himself he would undoubtedly have occasion to test those words in the future. He left the meeting impressed with Anslinger's offer but with strong misgivings about the effectiveness of a "police approach" to the problem. As a policeman's son he was no stranger to law enforcement procedures. But he was convinced that fingerprinting, wiretapping, marksmanship, handcuffs, search warrants and so on could not solve the problem of one weeping woman or one shattered life. On the other hand he was convinced that kindness, patience and tolerance could.

He considered his girls in the light of the theory that most addicts were criminals first and addicts later. The girls' own experiences seemed to refute this. Most, in fact, had become addicted while minors, when they could hardly be termed criminals. Many had certainly been tough, jungle-wise animals since childhood. As they matured they certainly developed into readily identifiable criminals—that is, thieves and prostitutes. But they did not commit crime to enjoy the usual pleasures of the proceeds. They committed crime only to buy drugs.

And what about the pushers, the small-time peddlers of drugs? Men and women charged with selling narcotics draw the fury of the city's judges and are damned as despicable and dangerous enemies of society. To the outsider this approach is unassailable. But, in nearly all cases, a pusher is nothing more than a junkie, driven by his insatiable needs and by the relentless blackmail of wholesalers to sell to others. In fact the most extreme addicts, hundred-dollar-a-day users, are usually the most active pushers.

Invariably, the addict somehow finds whatever income is needed to sustain his or her habit—until caught and jailed. Female addicts have three principal sources of income: prostitution, theft and drug selling. Yet curiously, within this framework, they observe a rigid code. Some addicts, through moral principle—or some past, nameless horror—never become prostitutes. But they can embark on a shoplifting orgy early in the day and walk out of a department store hours later stout and perspiring, wearing six dresses and numerous layers of underwear beneath their regular garments plus an eye-popping variety and quantity of other items concealed about them. Other girls disdain stealing; they might have to run too fast. Few girls are pushers. It is dangerous and the penalties are severe.

But crime is not all petty in the world of drugs. Father Egan was conscious that he moved in close proximity to one of the biggest, most efficiently organized and sinister criminal conspiracies in history. And while he felt compassion and sorrow for the addict, he had only anger for narcotics racketeers who never use drugs. In their case he sided emphatically with Commissioner Anslinger and other advocates of stern punishment.

His awareness of the vast, invisible traffic in drugs came to him through his girls. An expensively dressed prostitute arrived in the House and admitted she had an eighty-dollar-a-day heroin habit. She bragged she had no difficulty in finding the money.

"I can make five hundred in one day, if I want to take the chance. I don't *have* to hustle," she told him.

"Five hundred doing what?" he asked skeptically.

"Listen, all I got to do is pick up a package of heroin here and take it there."

"Where is 'here' and where is 'there'?"

She shook her red hair violently.

"Sorry, Father. I can't even tell *you* that. I'll just say I can knock on a door in one of the best apartment houses in town, on Park Avenue, and make five hundred in a hour. Just making a delivery across town. I could go to the door right now, if they'd let me, and bring back enough junk to keep everyone in this joint high for a month."

Father Egan asked the girl to cooperate with police in preparing a trap at the apartment. She looked at him in astonishment.

"Nothing doing, Father. You don't know these people. If I squealed I'd be dead twenty-four hours after I left this jail."

The racket is vast. Heroin reaches New York and the rest of the nation through a maze of international smuggling and intrigue. Its journey frequently begins in Middle Eastern and Balkan poppy fields. There the bulb of the poppy flower is milked, exuding crude opium in black, gumlike form. Illicit chemists convert this into morphine and ship it to clandestine laboratories in western Europe for further processing into heroin. From there it is smuggled into New York.

Between the poppy fields and the piers and airline ramps of New York the value of each consignment jumps sharply. In New York one kilo, or 35½ ounces, priced at three thousand dollars, can be sold for nine to ten thousand dollars, depending on current market values. At this stage it is uncut, or usually about 87 percent pure. Before reaching the addict on the streets, however, it is drastically diluted with milk sugar and quinine. Eventually, the original three-thousand-dollar kilo attains a retail value of three hundred thousand dollars and more.

About five thousand pounds of heroin are consumed annually in the United States, requiring for their production twelve metric tons of opium. This constitutes seven-tenths of one percent of the world's legal opium production and an unknown percentage of the vast illicit production. Consequently the volume of heroin reaching the United States is a tiny trickle from an immense supply.

Customs officers and others seeking to stem this flow face a staggering task. Heroin has been found embedded in canned food, in engines of airliners, jammed behind the steel plates of ship's hulls, in automobile headlights, in the possession of diplomats, in the false bottoms of immigrants' baggage—without the immigrants' knowledge—in women's underclothing and within the body itself. Once, when a waterfront strike forced many incoming vessels to lie at anchor instead of berthing at New York piers, the supply of heroin in the city noticeably dwindled within a few days.

From an informant Father Egan once received the astonishing information that heroin was being smuggled into the city from Europe inside the bodies of corpses being returned to their families.

"Some funeral parlor in Brooklyn is in it, Father," his caller told him. "I don't know which one, but I'll try to find out. I hear the dead guys are full of the stuff."

Father Egan thanked him and immediately dialed the Federal Bureau of Narcotics.

"The stiffs are loaded with junk," he said, "and that's all I know about it now. As soon as I hear more, you'll know about it."

But he heard no more. As often happened in the world in which he moved, his informant vanished without trace.

For years addiction and its associated problems had been a cause of serious concern to large numbers of public-spirited citizens in the city. Many of them were doctors, sociologists, politicians and lawyers. They held frequent meetings and forums to discuss the problem and ways of coping with it. Father Egan soon became a participant at many of these meetings, usually held in the auditoriums of community centers. He sat through lectures on the chemistry of addiction, on psychiatry, on medical treatment of addicts, on the complex pattern of varying state laws on addiction. The more meetings he attended, however, the more they contributed to his frustration. Such gatherings, he felt, were more concerned with the problem than they were with the people with the problem.

He took Corinne to one meeting and they sat side by side listening to a noted psychiatrist explaining childhood experiences that could lead to drug addiction in later life. The speaker concluded by inviting questions from the audience.

Father Egan nudged Corinne. "Ask him," he said, with steely humor, "if he's ever met a drug addict." Corinne looked at him in panic. "Go on," he commanded. Corinne's hand shot up and she haltingly asked the question.

The lecturer was silent for a few seconds as he rearranged

the papers on his podium. Finally he looked up and conceded he had not. No, he had never met or spoken to an addict.

"An honest man," Father Egan whispered to the girl, and Corinne giggled.

He took her to a cafeteria and as they munched hamburgers he reflected that the evening had not been wasted. In fact it supported a theory he had been evolving for some time. There was a missing link in the chain of the rehabilitation process. There were too many experts on addiction and too few dedicated people working in the field. To the experts, to professional people, the problem was a job. If they were not examining this problem they would be examining another. But this was not enough. There was no problem quite like this one. At 5 P.M. the problem did not disappear until the next day. The problems of addicts and prostitutes did not close down when offices closed down, when social welfare agencies closed for the weekend.

As he sipped his coffee, he looked at Corinne. She was plumper and more self-confident than on the night he had hauled her out of that apartment. Since then she had served one more stretch in the House of D. Or was it two? She was trying desperately, he knew, to stay away from drugs, and was maybe only just chippying a little, just taking a light shot now and then.

To save her there would have to be recruitment of people who lived in neighborhoods where drug taking was rife, where the problem of addiction could be dealt with on a practical basis. It was easy to be interested in the problem, but it wasn't easy to be interested in the people with the problem.

Who wanted to waste a morning trying to get an addict a job? Who would devote an evening to a bitter, needle-scarred thief and prostitute and encourage her, befriend her? How many would take a defeated human being in hand and help her recover her life?

5. THE JUNKIE PRIEST

1

ONE MORNING, out of half-a-dozen girls released from the House, he was able to find a job for one of them as a waitress. Her name was Anita and she had a police record of more than thirty arrests for narcotics, prostitution and theft. But she was, he knew, a good girl. She was also savagely bitter and deeply pessimistic about her future.

"They'll find out I'm a junkie an' a hustler an' they'll fire me, Father," she told him, fighting back tears. "I'll never make it in this rotten, dirty, lousy town. When I'm on drugs and when I'm hustling I got a good apartment and nice clothes an' everything. When I try to work an' stay clean, I got nothin'. The only time the sun shines for me is when I'm high."

But she was determined to try again. And Father Egan wondered how long she would last this time. She could vanish into the jungle by noon and be back in jail by evening without even trying.

Yet it did happen sometimes. He thought of the tough-talking, wisecracking twenty-year-old who had walked out of the jail six months ago and had not returned to drugs or prostitution since. She had held doggedly to her typist's job and handed him her paycheck each week. He doled out to her what he figured she needed—there were no arguments—and put the rest in her savings account. Now *she*, he thought, might make it. Maybe.

Later, as dusk gathered in the Village, he walked home. He was tired, as usual. He had been up since six. After prayers he had spent an hour on the phone waking up a dozen girls, reminding them to be at work on time. He had spent the rest of the morning in the jail and on the streets,

43

trudging up stairs with bags of groceries, redeeming pawn tickets and instructing girls to call him at a certain time at a certain coin telephone on Sixth Avenue to tell him how they had fared on a job application or an apartment hunt. Sometimes the calls would come, sometimes not.

When he reached home the usual stack of messages was waiting. He flipped through them: call a detective, hospitals, several girls and one distraught mother. He dialed the detective.

The officer's voice grated through the phone. "Yeah, Father. We arrested your little Anita again."

Father Egan winced. "Where?" he asked wearily.

"On Eightieth Street. She came out of the hotel with this jerk. They checked in as man and wife. He said she asked him for twenty. We had no choice. It was a clean bust."

Listening, Father Egan visualized the dismal scene: the four-dollar hotel lobby, the deadpan desk clerk and part-time pimp, the elevator creaking down and the jerk, whoever he was, stepping out with Anita; the detectives moving forward, the panic on the man's face and Anita's resigned shrug. Father Egan was so discouraged at Anita's failure that he became angry with the detective.

"The john," he asked, with deliberate innocence, "the guy with Anita—what did you do with him?"

The detective snorted in exasperation.

"Aw, Father, you know better than that. He may have to testify."

"I guess Anita twisted his arm," Father Egan pressed. "She forced the john to go to the room with her, huh?"

The detective's voice assumed injured dignity. "Father, I just called to let you know we got this pride and joy. Nobody *else* wants to know we got her."

Immediately Father Egan was sorry he had been sarcastic with the cop. Again he considered the bitter irony: Nobody ever did anything with the prostitute's client; society winked at this particular double standard.

"Yes, I know," he said quietly. "I'll see her in the morning. How is she?"

"Sick. But she'll live."

"Okay. Thanks and God bless you."

Father Egan thought for a moment about Anita. A small, doe-eyed, childish-looking jungle dweller, and one of the smoothest operators in the city. Her procedure was as squalid as it was simple. It consisted of convincing the gullible john that this was the first time she had resorted to making money in this fashion, and that she was forced to do so only because she was disastrously behind in her room rent. She would tell him she was nervous, that she wanted to go to her room alone and that he should follow her in five minutes. Naturally, she had to have the money first to guarantee he would show up. And while the john was ascending in the wheezing elevator Anita was skipping down the stairs and into the street, cash in hand.

But Father Egan knew the reason for her ruthlessness. Heroin burned and consumed her bony frame; she was a true, end-of-the-line junkie with a raging habit that devoured money at the rate of seventy-five dollars and more a day. And all at twenty-three years old with a grieving, horrified family.

He recalled the last time he had appeared in Women's Court on her behalf. The judge, new to prostitution and addiction, had received him in his private office and regarded him with an approving but slightly incredulous smile. It was the smile he encountered often, the puzzled grimace that said: *It's great of you to spend your time doing this kind of work, but do you really know who you are doing it for?* Smile or no smile, the judge had at least granted Anita a release on probation, care of Father Egan. He wondered how the judge would greet him in the morning. With a kindly, I-told-you-so smile, no doubt.

He turned to a penciled message that had been found, neatly folded, in the front door mailbox.

DEAR FATHER EGAN,

May I please see you at your convenience on a matter of importance to me. I have worked as a nurse's aid and am very interested in this kind of work. I have been off narcotics for several months now. Do you think it is possible you can get me this type of job. If so, please let me know.

Thank you kindly,
respectfully
MAUREEN JENNINGS

A telephone number was scrawled after the signature. He dialed it. No answer.

He worked through the evening until midnight; tragedy piled on tragedy, heartbreak on heartbreak. Finally he climbed to the softly lit chapel on the second floor and knelt in prayer. In the dimness his face was unlined and curiously youthful. He looked like a man who had lived only among gentleness instead of one who walked shoulder-deep in desperation. After a while he rose and continued up the stairs to his room on the fifth floor. He fell asleep instantly.

The telephone blasted him awake. He felt as if he had slept thirty seconds. But he was out of bed before his eyes had opened. The street outside was still and morning was a long way off; he had no wish to awaken the other sleeping priests in the house. There was little doubt, anyway, that the call was for him. His particular flock began its day at midnight.

Sleepily, he picked up the telephone in the hallway and heard a woman's voice, Spanish-accented and urgent.

"Father Egan?"

"Yes."

He did not ask the caller's name. He never asked.

"Jackie pretty sick. She call for you. You better get to Bellevue in a hurry. They pick her up unconscious on Broadway."

He knew only one Jackie, a barbiturate addict.

"Pills?" he asked uselessly.

"Overdose."

"Okay, I'll be right there. Thanks and God bless you."

The phone clicked dead. It was 2 A.M. Outside, the neon of the Mexican restaurant and the liquor store opposite the friars' residence had long been switched off. Street lamps cast lonely pools of light on the sidewalks. At Twenty-Third Street he ran the red light and peered about for a stray patrol car. But only a few taxis sped toward midtown as he turned east on Twenty-Sixth Street and headed for the river.

For Jackie to have taken an overdose, he thought, she must have swallowed an entire wholesale carton of pills. She had been using barbiturates for so long she should have built up the tolerance of a horse. As he drove, junkie talk for barbiturates floated through his mind: *goofballs, nembies, yellow jackets, redbirds, blue heavens, jelly beans.* Barbiturates brought calm and sleep to the upset and irritated—and could become as addictive as morphine. Cut off a barbiturate addict's supply and you courted anxiety, weakness, trembling and nausea. Left untreated, these symptons could swiftly degenerate into convulsions and insanity. And sometimes death. They were left untreated often enough, he thought grimly.

And Jackie? A beat-up, washed-out skinny blonde of twenty-four with bad teeth and a dishwater complexion. She looked as if she had been bounced off the wall of every jailhouse and precinct station from Perth Amboy to Bridgeport, and probably had. Her past was a wilderness, years of prostitution, drugs and hunger; her future was the same, if she had a future. In fact there was nothing certain about Jackie except that the state of her soul was not ready for her to meet her Maker. He pressed his foot down and the car sped forward on the one-way, crosstown street. *I must reach her before she dies,* he thought, *so she can make her peace with God. I don't care how often she's fallen as long as she comes back to God before she dies.*

He braked to a jolting halt at First Avenue, then eased the car across the street into Bellevue's emergency entrance. The driveway was normally used only by ambulances and hospital officials but the guard at the lighted gate recognized him and waved him on. Father Egan drove past the ambulance garage, swung left and halted in the parking lot. Bellevue's buildings towered above him, their windows ablaze. He strode through a side entrance into a high-ceilinged corridor and headed for the emergency ward.

The ward was hushed. He looked down at the first curtained bed and saw a brutally beaten derelict, his ragged clothes soaked in blood. The man kept trying to sit up, groaning, and a nurse kept gently pushing him back to the bed.

At the lower end of the ward an intern and a nurse stood beside a childlike figure that stirred beneath the sheets. Father Egan moved closer and saw it was Jackie. The girl lay face up, her colorless hair spread across the pillow. Her face was gray and deep shadows curved beneath her closed eyes. She looked old and fragile. Saliva dribbled from her pale lips and her breathing was faint. As he watched, she shuddered in a violent convulsion.

Stepping beside the young doctor, Father Egan spoke softly. "I know this girl, doctor. She's a friend of mine. This is Jackie, a well-known goofball addict."

The intern nodded. "Oh, I see. An addict."

"If you don't mind my giving a little advice," Father Egan continued casually, "I'd suggest we tip her up a bit. If we keep her head down it'll keep her mouth dry and she won't be swallowing all that saliva. We could elevate the foot of the bed and keep the nasopharynx clear of secretion. I can keep her awake with some light slapping and pinching while you give her a shot of about fifteen milligrams of benzedrine. That'll calm her. Some nikethamide should help, too. And the nurse can administer oxygen."

The doctor was staring at him inquiringly. Father Egan felt he was about to become embroiled in another argument with a doctor—they occurred occasionally—when an older physician, who had approached the bed silently, placed a light hand on his shoulder. The doctor peered at Jackie, then mildly surprised the intern by instructing him to follow Father Egan's advice.

"He knows as much about this as some of us," he confided.

The intern and nurse went to work and Father Egan watched as the hypodermic needle sank into Jackie's flaccid arm. She relaxed visibly and turned her head to the pillow, her face in sudden repose. After a while the intern nodded and stepped away from the bed.

"She's okay for now," he said. "At least she's out of danger."

Without asking anyone Father Egan opened Jackie's purse on the chair beside her bed. He rummaged through the comb, lipstick, Kleenex package and crumpled letters inside, searching for barbiturates. But Jackie evidently had used her supply. After a quick search of her coat pockets he left the ward.

The streets remained quiet. It was not yet 3 A.M. He drove slowly to the Village, obedient to red lights. When he got to bed the sight of Jackie, convulsing beneath the sheet, the skin on her face stretched tightly over her bones, remained with him a long time.

The first light of morning rose over Bellevue and filtered into the quickening streets of Manhattan before sleep came again.

2

Not all encounters with doctors had been so congenial. One brusque and efficient physician once curtly informed him that addicts did not belong in any hospital, that they should be made to "kick it in the streets, where they belonged." And there had been the memorable night when he had exploded at what he regarded as an attitude of unforgivable callousness.

He had arrived at the hospital to find a girl, a heroin addict, deep in the throes of withdrawal. She was curled in her bed, knees under her chin, vomiting helplessly. Each wrench of her body was accompanied by a dry, scraping croak that seemed to rise from the depths of her body. At the foot of the bed sat a young intern, studying her intently. Father Egan stood beside the bed for a few seconds, waiting for the doctor to act. Finally he had become angry.

"Doctor," he said, trying to control himself, "can't you do something for this girl instead of watching her as if she were an experiment in a glass cage?"

The doctor had cocked an eye at him.

"And just who," he asked coldly, "are you?"

Father Egan became furious. The girl was suffering, as only heroin addicts suffer, and this newcomer to the wards was bickering with him.

"Never mind who I am," he shot back. "I'm just wondering who you are. Maybe you ought to be driving a truck. Look at you, you're supposed to be a doctor and you're sitting here as if this girl were an exhibit. Haven't you ever seen a junkie before? She's not a criminal, she's sick!"

The doctor was outraged. He rose to his feet.

"And what are you?" he grated. *"A junkie priest?"*

It was the first time Father Egan had heard the term. But he was too exasperated, too concerned for the sweating girl on the bed for the words to register on him. Another doctor and some nurses placated him and whispered to the flushed intern. Others immediately attended to the addict. Within minutes she was sleeping comfortably.

As he strode from the ward a young nurse stopped him. He knew her well and had often marveled at her seeming imperviousness to the horrors of the emergency room.

"Father," she said quietly, "that was the nicest thing anyone could have said about you."

"What was?"

"The doctor calling you a junkie priest."

He laughed and thanked her. Her words, and the doctor's, were forgotten until a few days later when a call came from an addict, seeking help in finding a job. After that the words were never forgotten. The call was routine except for the fact that the caller did not ask to speak to Father Egan. She asked to speak to the Junkie Priest.

He decided at first it was a coincidence, or perhaps a joke. But when succeeding callers and girls he met in the prison and on the streets used the same term, he realized he had acquired a name uniquely his own. How, he was never sure. Perhaps the nurse had told others about the incident with the intern. Or had the junkie been listening? Addicts often remained strangely and acutely aware of their surroundings even in deepest misery. Had she, in the mysterious and indefinable way they had, transmitted the name to the underworld grapevine?

However it had been done, he was not displeased.

3

Since his earliest association with addiction Father Egan had become convinced that time was running out for him and that before he died he had to set in motion some mechanism of rehabilitation, some means of saving for society women who continually revolved in and out of jails.

He did this with the recognition that he was in no way indispensable to society and that when he died he would be quickly forgotten. He accepted the fact that there would always be crime, always prisons, always sin. But he emphatically refused to understand why, amid the vast material affluence of his country, no one had yet been able to arouse society's indignation over the plight of the women he knew.

It seemed inconceivable to him that no organization, no public body, no individual of influence, had stirred society's conscience to the extent of establishing a halfway house, an after-jail institution, for women in New York. What he envisioned was so humble when compared to the mighty building projects constantly under way in the city. All he wanted, as a beginning, was a sparely furnished old house where women could live for a few days, even weeks, when they left jail. It would be a home where they could rest in an atmosphere of kindness and dignity, where they could cook a meal, comb their hair and restore their courage.

The fact that this had not been done was proof enough to him that God wanted someone to do it. This was the reason for his adamant refusal to abandon his work among addicts even in the face of compelling arguments to do so. He could not begin to number the times he had been prey to serious doubts about the advisability and usefulness of carrying on. The temptation to quit had come not only from within—he traced this to the Devil—but from friends, including priests, who had tried to convince him of the futility of his activities. They asked him, again and again, why he insisted on wasting his time with people who did not appreciate either him or what he was trying to do, why he devoted himself to this lowest culture of society. He could achieve so much more, they reasoned, in other directions. Why try to help those who would return to sin immediately? They urged him to forget the problem of drug addiction as society's lost cause.

He listened—and returned to his junkies. He knew he might have been considered a greater success if, perhaps, he had concentrated on preaching. He could have done this, he figured, simply by returning to his early preoccupation with juvenile problems, by resuming his teen-age missions, worthy projects themselves.

He recalled his days as a missionary priest in North Carolina. When he had left there another priest had taken over his work and, he was sure, had done a better job. In fact, in preaching any mission, in teaching in a seminary, or in carrying out any assignment, other priests could do as well as he, and better. But here, deep in the subculture of prostitution, drug addiction and female crime, it was different. At night, when he knelt in prayer, he asked himself, without a vestige of pride, who would work among his addicts, his junkies, if he did not?

It was true that the problem in New York was so vast that whatever he did seemed hardly to mark the surface of the total evil. But at least there were those to whom he could bring some comfort, some help. And he knew, with conviction born of bitter experience, that if he did not do so, no one else would.

There were no statistics to prove the value of his work. If he had been seeking to establish a statistical accounting of his efforts—such as the number cured of addiction over the number he had counseled—he knew he could be judged a failure. He kept no such figures. But he was not searching only for those kinds of results; he sought salvation of human souls. He knew if he did not believe the salvation of a single junkie's soul was above any other value, he could not have persevered so long. He could not, in fact, have become a priest. If only some of his girls, even one of them, saw in his actions the mercy of God and thus came back to Him before they died, then it was all worth while.

Yet he could not be content with this. He had to be an instrument of God in opening a halfway house, a junkies' haven. He could not continue aiding the individual addict on the assumption that a trend of sociological thinking was turning in favor of the halfway house idea, that such an institution would be established one day anyway, with or without his help. He had to exert pressure on public officials, he had to fight. He was thankful that his superiors also realized this; for in many cases his missions, his other duties as priest, were conveniently scheduled to enable him to pursue his work among addicts.

It was a happy life, he reflected. When a girl came to him late at night and told him she had not eaten that day, that she had no place to live, there was considerable happiness to be found in providing her with a week's rent, even if he knew she was heading back to prostitution the next day. If he could keep her out of sin for a single night, let alone a week, he was achieving a great deal. That was why he often took two or three girls to a movie, or a ride on the Staten Island Ferry. At least it kept them off the streets for a couple of hours.

And sometimes, as in the case of Carol, he even had a statistic.

6. CAROL

1

CAROL WAS one of scores, even hundreds, of girls Father Egan found who had become addicted in their teens. As a fifteen-year-old in an Ohio town she had attended the usual party, met the usual wrong youth, and taken the first terrible fix in a bathroom, while the record player blared in the living room.

"I was a kid," she told him, "and this guy dared me to take it. My ma and pa were drunk an' fightin' all the time. All I wanted was to be liked by someone, and this guy with his needle had to be it."

So at fifteen Carol began to use heroin. The boy friend occasionally provided her with some in return for delivering small packages of the drug to certain addresses throughout the city. No one suspected a gray-eyed, full-cheeked blonde schoolgirl in a pony tail to be part of a rapidly growing narcotics operation dominated by gangsters.

"I wasn't even addicted at first," she said. "But about a month later, after injecting maybe a couple of times a week, I woke up feelin' uncomfortable. You know, my joints ached, my nose was running and I was nauseated. I told mother I had a virus and that I was stayin' home from school. I took a shot in the bathroom and felt great; I figured that whatever was wrong with me, heroin was the cure. The next morning, though, I felt just as bad. So I took my needle to school with me, and took a shot between classes. I used to look around at the other kids and sing to myself: *'I got a secret.'* "

But as her need for the drug grew, Carol begged for more from her boy friend, the up-and-coming pusher. In reply he had beaten her almost unconscious and had thrown her out of his hotel room, threatening to kill her if she breathed a word about what she knew.

"You want any stuff," he snarled at her, "you pay for it. I shoulda known in the first place not to have anything to do with a dumb kid who ain't got the sense not to get herself hooked. If you don't know how to make a buck, there's plenty of girls who can show you what to do. Now beat it."

Carol, now obviously a sick girl even to her mother's alcohol-blurred gaze, became desperate. She had to have money from somewhere. As a child she had sometimes stolen lipsticks and other small items from stores. This time she tried to steal a heavy winter coat and was immediately caught. Adjudged a wayward child, she was sent to a reformatory. On leaving the institution three years later she became a prostitute, easily earning enough to satisfy her twenty-dollar-a-day heroin habit. Aged eighteen, Carol packed a suitcase and never saw her home or parents again.

To Carol, heroin became as essential as air and water. The drug took possession of her mind and body, unbalancing her metabolic processes and gearing them to its influence. Without the drug, she felt, she would literally fly apart. Theft and prostitution, to assure a large and steady income, became a deadly necessity.

But Carol became swept up in a rising public clamor to eliminate the drug traffic in the state. Early in the nineteen-fifties the legislature responded to this by authorizing a full-scale study of the narcotic situation. Finally, in 1955, the blow fell. A law calling for a two- to ten-year prison sentence for illegal possession of drugs was passed. The penalty for such possession with *intent* to sell became ten to forty years —and for actual, illegal sale, twenty to forty years. The Federal Narcotics Bureau claimed this legislation "broke the back of the narcotics racket in Ohio." The bureau added that drug violations plummeted by 80 percent and that its force of agents in the state was safely reduced from twenty to three.

Other states also were placing harsh statutes on their books to cope with the narcotics problem. Louisiana approved penalties of thirty to ninety-nine years—without probation, parole or suspension of sentences—for any person older than twenty-one who conveyed a narcotic drug to anyone under twenty-one.

In Ohio, at least, this type of legislation threw many addicts into panic, forcing them to flee the state. One of these was Carol. Terrified at the severity of the new laws, especially those striking at mere possession of drugs, Carol fled to New York.

When she arrived, Father Egan had been working among addicts for a little more than three years.

2

Carol was twenty-three when she came to the city, a tall, earthily attractive girl with only the beginnings of the ravages of drugs and prostitution showing on her broad, fair-skinned features. She gravitated almost immediately to a ten-dollar-a-week room in a West Side slum known as San Juan Hill.

Years later, the neighborhood, centering on Sixty-Fourth Street and Broadway, was to house the complex of buildings known as the Lincoln Center for the Performing Arts. But when Carol arrived there it was a sore even on New York's decaying West Side skin. Trash sailed out of upper-floor windows, children heaved bricks from rooftops, drunks staggered and vomited on the sidewalks, and petty hoodlums, switchblade knives in hand, lurked in garbage-strewn hallways. The junkies used foul hallway bathrooms as "shooting galleries." Heroin, clean and strong, was readily available everywhere; it was also expensive, Carol recalled.

"I had reached my last few dollars and I had a habit costing me, oh, about twenty or thirty dollars a day. So I asked around, here and there, and soon learned that I would have little trouble in making that much. After a few weeks I hustled on a steady corner on Seventh Avenue, near Times Square."

She lived only to acquire enough money for drugs; nothing repelled her. But New York, or rather the restless, shifting area in which she plied her trade, did seem to have more than its fair share of the offbeat.

"The creeps I met!" she said. "Where do they come from? Some of them were animals, not people. Do you know what happened to me one night? I returned to a hotel with a short, heavy guy who just nodded to me without saying anything. As soon as we got into the room and locked the door he hauled off and knocked me clear across the room, then picked me up and started hitting me again. When I asked him what he was doing it for, he said he hated women like me. Then he really tried to kill me.

"He almost shoved me out of the window—the room was four floors over the street and I could see the people and the lights below—but he shifted his grip to get a better hold and I managed to break loose and get out of there. That night, I can tell you, I went straight home and cried."

The following night Carol was arrested in New York for the first time. A curly-haired youth in a sports shirt, speaking with a strong Irish brogue, had pestered her for hours as she came and went with her clients throughout the evening. But after the sixth customer Carol decided to go home; she was still shattered by the previous evening's experience. Her night's take was ninety dollars and it would have to do. But the Irishman was persistent—he flashed seaman's papers and a thick roll of bills as he leered at her cheerfully. Carol hesitated, and was tempted. She nodded. But once inside the room, when she asked for twenty dollars, the Irish brogue—and the cheerfulness—vanished. Instead the youth pulled a shiny badge from his pocket.

"Police," he said. "You're under arrest."

Carol looked at him in disbelief.

"You're kidding," she said.

"Let's go," he replied, not unkindly.

"You mean you went to all that trouble, standing there all those hours, over *me?*"

"Let's go."

The guards at the House of Detention took one look at Carol, noted her watering eyes and mild twitching, and conducted her into the tank. Carol's withdrawal symptoms were violent and she spent the first night in the tiny cell curled into a ball, a whimpering, agonized, sleepless wretch.

When she appeared in Women's Court in the morning she shuffled to the bench with her uncombed head down, oblivious to her surroundings. She neither knew nor cared what was being said by the judge or the prosecuting attorney or the young detective who had arrested her. She merely realized, dimly, that she was being sentenced to sixty days in jail for prostitution.

Back at the House she threw herself on her cot again and waited, animal-like, for the sickness to pass. The House terrified her. It was different from the open-air-type reformatory she had known at home; here was nothing but tier upon tier of steel-barred cells and an endless clanging of iron. Even the open-air recreation area on the prison's roof was encompassed by a net of thin steel.

The sixty days passed like a troubled dream and Carol found herself one bright morning on the sidewalk outside the jail. By the curb, in deep conversation with a girl who had been released earlier in the morning, stood a slight, gray-haired priest. Carol wondered idly what a priest was doing talking to this particular girl, an addict-prostitute like herself. But she forgot about him on the subway ride uptown.

Before entering her small room, with its window looking out on a trash-piled backyard, Carol begged a shot of heroin from a junkie seated on the building's front steps, enjoying the midday sunshine. In her room, she quickly sank into a yawning, nodding indolence as the drug banished pain, care and memory from her mind.

Years passed for Carol in much the same manner on the New York streets. She paced the sidewalk on Seventh Avenue as the city's seasons changed from snowy winters to steaming summers. She became known as "the big blonde with the big habit," and her life turned only on a wheel of addiction, prostitution and jail.

"I'm in and out of that old House of D. so often," she remarked sadly one day to an expressionless police sergeant, "you guys oughta gimme my own key."

Carol was sad because her figure had shrunk from malnutrition, her once lustrous hair had become thin and wispy, her teeth were discolored and her voice was a husky rasp. She was a mess and she knew it. She was a junkie and there was nothing that could be done about it.

"Every once in a while I used to hear about a priest who gave a helping hand to girls like me," she recalled later, "and I would remember the priest standing outside the House of D. one morning when I got out. But then I'd forget about it. Anyway, it seemed to make no difference. I chose the life I was leading and it was up to me to make the best of it. It was rough sometimes, though."

A lean youth in a brown suit winked at her and tugged at her arm at 2 A.M. one night. But she shook him off contemptuously. Who did he think she was? He even *looked* like a greenhorn cop posing as an out-of-town visitor. He wasn't going to find anything to arrest her for that way. But it was no use.

As she continued walking on the street, ignoring him, he caught up with her and grabbed her arm.

"You're under arrest," he snapped.

"For what?" she demanded.

"Soliciting."

Usually she knew better than to argue, but lately her temper and self-control were beginning to slip. This time she exploded.

"What's the matter with you?" she yelled, causing passers-by to stop and stare. "Didn't you make your quota tonight? Is the lieutenant gettin' on your back because you're not makin' enough arrests? And you figure it doesn't make any difference to me anyway?"

The detective's face was stony.

"Shut up," he said, "and let's go."

Another ninety days in the House of D.

Where, Carol wondered, was the little girl who had gone to that party in Ohio so long ago? On leaving the prison she thought miserably of the ruin she had made of her life. This depressed her so much that there was only one thing she could think of to make the day bearable: drugs.

The perfect spring afternoon mellowed into evening and the edges of the city's buildings merged into the darkening sky, leaving only thousands of windows sparkling in the night. On Upper Broadway, where Carol emerged from the subway, the sidewalks were thronged and old people sat on benches and read newspapers by neon light.

It was a Friday evening, and for Carol a lost, but significant, weekend was about to begin.

Near Ninety-Sixth Street she wandered into an all-night cafeteria and a pockmarked youth nodded to her in recognition. She sat down heavily at his table.

"Got any?" she asked wearily.

"A few."

"I only got two bucks."

"Fifty cents each."

"Gimme four for a dollar."

"I give eight for two dollars."

The deal was made and swiftly the barbiturate pills changed hands. Carol swallowed two of the pills and felt her body and spirits revive. In a lunch counter on the west side of Broadway she propositioned a middle-aged man and led him to her small room. Soon she was ten dollars richer. Carol then walked east to an apartment house, located above a row of dilapidated stores on Amsterdam Avenue, and rapped briskly on a second-floor door. She waved the ten-dollar bill like an admission ticket and purchased a package of heroin, borrowing a needle and using it there. Next she returned to the cafeteria near Ninety-Sixth Street and bought more barbiturates with the change from the ten dollars.

She laughed and sang a little to herself. It was late now and she sat at a corner table for hours, nodding and gabbing with other addicts who walked constantly in and out, each on an unknown assignation.

A gray dawn rose over near-deserted Broadway. Carol lifted a tired head as a night watchman entered the cafeteria for his morning coffee. She sidled up to him and looked at him questioningly. He nodded assent, accompanied her to her room, and Carol soon had another twelve dollars.

Later she ran into a thin, lugubrious addict she knew as José. As he approached her on the street she whooped at him.

"Hey José!" she cackled, her voice cracked and high-pitched. "Let's go. I got enough for both of us!"

She beamed at him as a smile broke over his sallow face. Carol and José soon spent her twelve dollars on heroin and found a bare room in a condemned tenement building where they could rest until the effect of the drug subsided. They sat on the dusty floor until noon, talking idly.

As sunlight slanted through the room's uncurtained windows Carol rose and left José. He did not look up as she walked out. He merely sat quietly, a black-haired youth with his head bent low and his hands clasped about his knees.

On the sidewalk, Carol halted for a moment. What day was this, she asked herself, Saturday or Sunday? She decided it was Saturday and walked on. Within a block, on Columbus Avenue, she ran into two more junkies, loping along the sidewalk like stray dogs. Without breaking stride they led her to a room on West Eighty-Fourth Street where they purchased five dollars' worth of heroin, sharing the needle with her. Carol dozed off in a stuffed armchair. No one bothered her, and she slept through the day and night, her face chalk-white and slack-jawed. When she awoke the sun was high. Yawning, she crammed a few goofballs into her mouth and wandered again into the street. The usually busy sidewalks were hushed and it was only when Carol observed stacks of newspapers piled around a corner newsstand that she realized it was Sunday morning.

Without particular reason she headed back to Broadway and Ninety-Sixth Street. As she walked the sun became shadowed by fast-moving clouds and soon a light rain began to fall, quickening into a deluge.

Carol gazed about the washed, gleaming street, feeling only vaguely the refreshing caress of the rain on her cracked, parched skin. Befuddled with drugs, she leaned for a moment against a poster-covered wall, intending to rest for a few minutes.

She remained standing there for hours, the rain streaming down her gaunt and aging face.

3

By Monday morning Carol was utterly abject. She felt ill, tired and desperately alone. She had not changed her clothes in three days.

"That morning," she was later to tell Father Egan, "I felt I had hit bottom. The thought of staying alone in my little room scared me; I knew I would have to run and get a fix in fifteen minutes if I did that. And I was sick and tired of the whole thing. It was the first time in my life I had felt that way. All I wanted to do was to sit around and talk with someone, with a friend. And I realized that after all my years in New York I didn't know one person I could do that with. In fact even the girls I knew were all in the House of D. So I actually went downtown to see if I could spot one of them."

She walked up and down on the sidewalk outside the prison, feeling its bulk towering above her and staring up at its rows of windows.

And suddenly she heard a voice cry her name. Desperately she looked from window to window, then heard the cry again. As her sunken, shadowed eyes darted over the building she saw a hand wave from the top floor, then release a small object which sailed down to fall lightly at her feet.

She bent and picked it up; it was a tightly wadded piece of paper. Carol opened it and read the penciled words:

See Father Egan, 138 Waverly Place, Greenwich Village.

Carol looked at the message dumbly. She knew no Father Egan. Her circle of acquaintances did not exactly include a priest, as she assumed he was. But she recalled the rumors about a priest helping junkies and remembered the black-clad figure she had once seen on this same sidewalk. She shrugged. She was finished anyway; in a few hours she would be desperately in need of heroin and would do anything to get it. She would inevitably be arrested again and return to this prison. Nothing would change and she had nothing to lose.

Father Egan had just finished Mass when he heard the bell ring. He descended the stairs clad in his friar's habit and opened the front door.

He leveled one shrewd glance at Carol and beckoned her inside to a small reception room off the hallway.

He smiled at her. "Have a seat," he said.

Silently, Carol handed him the note. She looked speculatively at this slim man in an ankle-length robe and lifted her shoulders slightly. Father Egan noted the shrug while reading the message; he observed the note was written on the same kind of paper, folded in the same manner, as the messages he found every day in his envelope at the jail.

"Are you this Father Egan?" Carol croaked.

"There may be other Father Egans. Which one do you want?"

"Would anyone in the House of D. know you?"

"One or two. How about some coffee?"

She nodded. When Father Egan brought her the coffee and lit her a cigarette he eyed her worn clothing, stringy hair and stockingless legs. The girl was twitching slightly and he figured she had taken her last fix from twelve to twenty-four hours before. A bad enough case, he thought, one that needed detoxification quickly, or soon she would have to go back uptown for more drugs.

"Sick, huh?" he asked.

Carol eyed him carefully. Only her friends used that expression in quite the same way. What kind of a priest was this?

"Real sick," she replied.

"Tired?"

Carol's eyebrows rose slightly. He had used another junkie term, the word that meant an addict had finally had enough. She nodded.

"How tired?"

"I'll do anything."

"I'd like you to take a rest—in hospital."

Her shoulders rose in her familiar shrug.

"Wait here," he said. "I'll make a phone call."

In the hallway he dialed Bellevue Hospital.

"How many addicts do you have today?" he asked the admissions office.

"Four, Father. The quota."

"Okay, can you switch me to the supervisor's office?"

"Sure."

To one of Bellevue's senior officers Father Egan explained that, in his opinion, he had a case in immediate need of hospitalization.

"Good enough," the doctor said. "Bring her in. I'll call down and let 'em know you're coming."

Father Egan hung up with some gratification. The doctor's response was another payoff for the indignation, pleading and arguing that had characterized his activities since he encountered his first addict, now long ago. Slowly and gradually, he had found, doctors and nurses were changing their attitude toward addicts and were treating them as sick people, no more or less.

Thirty minutes later Carol and Father Egan walked into Bellevue. She accompanied him submissively. Carol could not tell herself why, but she trusted this little guy. He had not preached at her, had not even been excessively sympathetic. Being with this priest was almost like being with another junkie.

A nurse greeted them. "How's the Junkie Priest?" she asked.

"Busy."

Startled, Carol looked sideways at Father Egan. The Junkie Priest?

Father Egan turned to the intern on duty. "This girl's a heroin addict, doctor. Her withdrawal will probably be severe."

The doctor nodded, noting the information on Carol's chart.

After Carol was in bed, Father Egan sat beside her. He asked about her home and whether she had a family.

"I ain't seen my family since I was a kid," Carol said flatly and without regret. "I got an uncle somewheres in Oregon, in Portland. Only I ain't seen him either since I was little. He used to bring me presents."

"Friends?"

"Junkies."

He gave her a packet of cigarettes and slipped two dollars into the drawer of her bedside table. He stood up and told her he would be back to see her later that evening.

"You sure you'll be back, Father?"

"I'm sure."

She watched him leave the ward, then sighed and pressed her face to the clean, cool pillow. When Father Egan returned that evening Carol was in deep withdrawal. Methadone had been administered but she was very ill. She had vomited incessantly for hours and was now exhausted and drowsy. She barely nodded to him as he sat down.

"Just try to get over tonight," he whispered. "Make it through the night and you'll feel better tomorrow."

This night would be the crucial time for Carol, he knew. It was the time when some addicts became so desperate for drugs that they signed themselves out of the hospital. The hospital could not detain them. Carol said nothing and just stared at him. In the morning, he came to her bedside again. Carol lay shivering and sweating under a mound of blankets. At least, he thought, she wasn't in jail, or on the streets, or looking for a fix. Or in the morgue.

"Panic on outside," he lied crisply. "Drugs are scarce. You're better off in here. At least you're getting methadone, and that's something. And it's better than cold turkey."

"Yeah."

"Feel better?"

"I can keep coffee on my stomach."

He paused. She would be detoxified, physically cured of addiction, within a few days. Then?

"You know being sick here could be a blessing," he told her. "It could give you time to do a little thinking."

"Hope so, Father."

"Maybe you'll realize you've really had it this time."

"It's about time." Carol began to cry softly. "I don't want to live this way any more," she whimpered, "one day to the next. In jail, outa jail. Hustlin', shootin' dope. I never felt this way before. I never cared. It was a life I picked out and I accepted it. Nobody's fault but mine."

He soothed her, told her not to harbor guilt feelings.

"I'm gettin' scared now," she continued. "I'm old before my time. I look at people who live normal and I look at myself an' I want to die. I can't look for a job. I don't know how to do anything. I got nothin' to put on an application form. All I got is needle marks up and down both arms. So when I think about it I got to take a shot just to feel better."

"It may be a good thing," Father Egan told her, "to think how your life has been wasted. Maybe you ought to pray to stay sick for a while so you'll really remember it when you feel better. Remember, you could have been arrested again. You could have died of an overdose."

Carol sobbed. "I don't wanna die. I wish I had a home an' a family. I wish I had a baby. . . ."

He sat and talked with her for a long time. Carol told him of her childhood, of the house party where she had taken her first fix, of her life since she had come to New York. They talked, as professionals, of drugs.

"Just garbage is all we're gettin', Father. Tough to get real high."

"Yes, I know. It's pretty weak stuff these days."

"Not worth goin' uptown to get it."

"Used to be strong, a year or so back."

"Sure was good."

When it was time for him to leave she was sitting up in bed, talking earnestly. That evening he was too busy to see her but he returned the following evening at 9:30. She looked at him reproachfully. "Father, I didn't see you a whole day."

"Sorry. Are you eating?"

"Yeah. Startin' to chuck. Eating all they give me."

"Anything I can get you? Cigarettes?"

"No, I got plenty. I bought them with the money you left me."

"Anything special you'd like?"

Carol smiled. It was the first time he had seen her do this. It delighted him. She leaned back on her pillow and closed her eyes.

"You know, Father," she said slowly. "I feel jus' like one of those pregnant women who want to eat one certain thing. I been thinking all evening I'd just like to sink my teeth into a big, cold apple. Gee, if only I had a real cold apple." She opened her eyes, and smiled again, shamefacedly.

"I'll get you one," he said.

As he spoke, Father Egan realized he might have talked too soon. It was almost 10 P.M. and where would he find an apple? But he had to keep his promise. He stood up. "Don't go away," he said. "I'll be back."

Outside, First Avenue was dark except for street lights. But further south, toward the Lower East Side, fruit trucks were parked bumper to bumper and he spotted a light in the rear of a small supermarket. He banged on the front door, but there was no answer. A driveway led to the rear and Father Egan cautiously felt his way through the darkness. Through a rear door window he saw a heavy man seated at a desk. Father Egan drew a coin from his pocket and tapped lightly on the glass. The man stood up, alarmed.

"Who there?" he shouted in a heavy accent. "Who knock? It's late. All closed. Come tomorrow."

An Italian, Father Egan thought. Maybe he's a Catholic. "Open up for a minute," he shouted back. "I'll explain."

The storekeeper peered through the glass. When he saw the priest's Roman collar he jumped visibly and opened the door. "Whatsa matter, Father? Why you come to the back?"

"The front was closed."

"It's late. Something is wrong, no?"

"No. I want an apple."

The storekeeper was stupefied. "An *apple?*"

"One apple. There's a sick woman in Bellevue and she wants an apple."

The storekeeper relaxed, although he still looked at Father Egan with amazement. "I give a whole case," he offered.

"I can't carry a whole case."

"Take six."

"Okay, six."

Father Egan returned to the hospital ward. It was dark and quiet and Carol seemed to be asleep. He nudged her pillow and when she opened her eyes he held out the apple. It felt icy in his hand. Carol lay still for a moment, her yellowish skin framed by the crisp whiteness of the pillow. Her eyes were bright and clear.

"It's a real apple," he whispered. "And it's cold and fresh."

Carol said nothing. She turned, placing her head on her right hand. With her left she took the apple from him and gently sank her teeth into it. She closed her eyes.

"Oh, it's so good, Father," she breathed. "So good."

"Here's a bagful. I have to go now."

As he stood up Carol shook her head. She was composed and serious. "Wait please, Father. Can I ask ya somethin'?"

"Sure."

"Why do this for me?"

"Do what?"

"Why bring me this apple?"

"Because you asked for it."

"But it's late. Everywhere's closed."

"I found a place."

"But why go to all that trouble?"

"I told you. You asked for it. It wasn't much to ask. You're a sick girl and if that's what you wanted, why not?"

"Father, you're a Catholic priest. You don't even know whether I'm Catholic or what I am."

Father Egan sat down again.

"Listen, Carol," he said quietly, "you're a sick girl, a human being and you've got dignity. And you're priceless in God's eyes. Always remember that."

Carol sank her head to the pillow. Tears glistened on her cheeks. "I don't get it," she said chokingly, "and I'll never get it. After all I told you. But I don't think you're going to regret it."

"You want to pay me for the apple?"

Carol nodded.

"Just make good. That's all. Now I have to go. It's getting late. Oh, one more thing. Give me the name and address of that uncle in Portland."

"Why?"

"I don't know yet. Give it to me anyway."

Carol gave him the name plus an old address she had carried for years. The following day, instead of heading directly to Bellevue, he visited the offices of the New York City Department of Welfare. He held a long conversation with a thoughtful caseworker at the department's division of transportation. How much money, he wanted to know, would be the limit the department would go to get Carol out of New York and give her a new start somewhere else?

Taking a chance, he sent a telegram to the address Carol had given him, asking her uncle to telephone him collect in New York. Within hours the call came. Father Egan drew a deep breath and explained Carol's plight, omitting nothing.

"You're the only person she says she knows outside New York," he said. "I've got to get her out of town. Can you help her find a place to live and maybe try to get her a job?"

The answer was clear over the thousands of miles of telephone line. "Sure, sure I will. You send her here. We'll take good care of her. We've got an extra room and she'll be welcome."

Father Egan sighed. "God bless you," he said. "Now, will you send me a telegram to that effect? Something I can show to get some money for her?"

"It's on the way."

Father Egan took the telegram to the Welfare Department. The department wired the uncle again to obtain written assurance that he would accept Carol.

When Carol was ready to leave the hospital Father Egan told her of his conversation with her uncle. She listened quietly, then nodded. "You're right, Father," she said. "I'll never make it here. Whatever you want me to do, I'll do."

The Welfare Department and Father Egan together bought Carol a one-way bus ticket to Portland. She was nervous when she boarded the bus and watched Father Egan wave as the vehicle pulled out of the terminal. It was worth a try, he thought. But would she be back in a week? Would he walk into the House of Detention and see her there? Two weeks later a letter came. He saw the Portland postmark and ripped it open quickly.

DEAR FATHER EGAN:

Please forgive me for not writing you sooner. I have been so busy, what with a new place to live and all. I feel good and have my fingers crossed. No junkies around here or if there are I don't know them and that's good. If I wanted to I would not know where to go for you know what. I got a room to myself. These people are treating me really swell. I don't want to let them down nor do I want to let you down. You been too good to me and I want to thank you very sincerely. I don't have a job yet but I hope maybe something will turn up soon.

> Yours very truly,
> CAROL

Father Egan whistled to himself. So far so good.

The months passed, with Carol occasionally returning to his mind. Christmas neared and he found several cards in his mailbox each day. They came from girls in the House, from the hospital at Lexington, from Bellevue and other hospitals and addresses throughout the city. Finally one came from Portland, a small card with a floral design. Carefully written inside was:

FATHER,

I pray for you all the time so I know you'll be all right. I owe so much to you. Thanks for giving me back my life.

> CAROL

At the House of Detention he passed it around.

"Look, I got a card from Carol."

Then he slapped his hat on his head and walked out. It was Wednesday night and he had a date at the YMCA.

7. WEDNESDAY NIGHT AT THE Y

HE STOOD silently for a moment, observing his audience. Two ex-prizefighters, a girl to whom life had never given a chance, a nail-biting youth, a resigned middle-aged prostitute, two expressionless penitentiary candidates and a pair of fresh-cheeked teen-agers still in nursing school.

Father Egan leaned casually against the table, its surface bare except for the propped-up card on which was printed: GOD GRANT ME THE SERENITY TO ACCEPT THE THINGS I CANNOT CHANGE, COURAGE TO CHANGE THE THINGS I CAN, AND THE WISDOM TO KNOW THE DIFFERENCE.

The small room was depressing. It contained four rows of hard chairs divided by a center aisle, a blackboard and a piano with a lid secured by a heavy padlock, and the table. The walls were painted a muddy beige.

The Wednesday night meeting of Narcotics Anonymous was in session.

Father Egan began slowly.

"Whatever you may think of yourself," he said, "you're a human being as far as God is concerned, a human being with dignity. You may have lost sight of that dignity doing the things you have to do to get junk. But it's something to be conscious of no matter how low you sink. Remember it when you're waiting on the corner for your fix, when you're on the streets hustling, when you're snatching someone's pocketbook, when you're busted in jail, when you're kicking it cold turkey."

He hoped he had captured his audience with these words, by injecting them with a single, back-straightening dose of pride.

This bitterly cold winter's evening, as on other Wednesdays throughout the year, he had taken the subway up to Twenty-Third Street from the Village and emerged near the old YMCA building half a block west of Seventh Avenue.

Even that half block, in freezing weather, was sufficient for
the usual sidewalk scenes to be enacted. Two or three shivering, tattered drunks offered him stupendous greetings as
he passed, rendering mighty doffs-of-the-hat and croaks of
"Good evenin' to ya, Father, good to see ya again this evenin', ya lookin' great."

Entering the Y's swinging doors and feeling the welcome
warmth on his face, Father Egan briefly noted the evening's
bulletin board.

WEDNESDAY

6:00	Country Dances	Rm. 304
6:30	Bridge Class	218
7:00	Modern Dance	202
8:00	American Camping Assn.	AUD.
8:30	NA	216

NA. Narcotics Anonymous. He checked his watch; it was
just 8:30 and he walked through the brightly lit lobby,
climbed the stairs to the second floor and entered Room 216.
Nodding to Rae Lopez, a dark-haired woman seated behind
the table, he sat down and greeted a Negro girl seated beside
him, her face masked by dark glasses.

"Hi, Della, you're early tonight."

"Yeah, Father, I had absolutely nothin' to do, so I thought
I'd jus' come an' set awhile."

"Good. Still clean?"

"So far."

"That's good. Keep it up."

He turned his head as two neatly dressed teen-aged girls
entered the room. They didn't *look* like junkies, but you
never know. One of them spotted his Roman collar and asked
diffidently, "Can we come in and listen? We're student
nurses from Bellevue."

"Sure, sit down. Anybody's welcome."

Seated now before the table were a lean, sandy-haired ex-
professional fighter dressed in sweater and, though it was
January, thin khaki pants; a dapper, thin-mustached youth
in dark suit and gleaming white shirt, chewing nervously on

a thumbnail; two silent Puerto Rican youngsters in the rear row; a red-haired, shapeless woman whose eyes were sunken, lusterless pits; the two student nurses; Della and Father Egan. With a soft tap on the door another youth entered. He swept the room with a swift glance, then walked with catlike steps to the first row of chairs and sat down. He wore an army field jacket and corduroy pants; his face was lean and taut. A white scar traced a harsh line from his left eyebrow to his chin.

Rae Lopez stood up. "Let's get started," she said, speaking in a slight Spanish accent. "Everybody get up and say the prayer." She pointed to the card propped on the table.

The scarfaced youth shook his head, grinning. "I don't go for no prayers," he explained. "I jus' came in to see what was happenin'. I been a fighter in the ring an' the only thing I'm prayin' for is a slow count." He looked around for laughs. There were none. The other ex-fighter looked at him wearily.

"All right, so you don't go for prayers," Rae Lopez replied tersely. "But we do. Good to see you here, anyway."

Father Egan smiled to himself. Rae knew precisely how to respond to the most unsure of addicts, as this newcomer almost certainly was.

The little gathering, with the scarred youth joining them in some embarrassment, rose and intoned the short prayer, then returned to their seats.

"For those who are newcomers tonight," Rae said brusquely, "welcome to the New York City chapter of Narcotics Anonymous. NA is patterned after Alcoholics Anonymous. We believe that alcoholism and addiction are basically the same and have found the AA program can be applied to our problem. However, because there are differences in the two problems we have had to modify the AA program to meet our needs. But just as a member of AA will tell you that only an ex-alcoholic can truly help the sick alcoholic, so we have learned that only an ex-addict can fully help the addict. We believe that by doing so we can regain our health and sanity. The only requirement for membership is an honest desire to stay free of drugs. Any questions?" She paused, then continued. "Tonight Father Egan, our chaplain, is here. Most of you know him. We will hear from him first."

Father Egan rose from his chair, walked to the table and faced the few seated people. As always he was deeply conscious of the peculiar pathos of the occasion. Here was a strange meeting in a lonely back room, a gathering remote from the city outside. Almost none of the city's millions even knew of the existence of NA. Yet the junkies drifted in each Wednesday night, some furtively, some desperately, some pretending to read magazines in the lobby while waiting for the meeting to begin. In all of New York, outside of a prison's wall, it was perhaps the only room where addicts could gather without shame or fear. He wondered what he could say to them, after the first few words he so fervently hoped would help raise their heads.

Somehow the words flowed effortlessly, buoyed by the intensity of his feeling.

"Sure, you feel like giving up," he cried. "Sure you say to yourself, 'What's the use of trying? I'm hopeless, I'm a junkie, and once a junkie always a junkie.' But, believe me, no human being is hopeless unless he completely despairs and gives up. I'm trying to say that unless you've got a pretty strong constitution and an even stronger desire, you certainly are *helpless* to help yourself once your whole physical system craves drugs. But even then you're not *hopeless* and far from it. Because you can take a cure and become physically detoxified so that your *body* doesn't need it. *Then you're in the position to help yourself.*"

He stopped, nodding to each face before him.

"And unless you can do that," he said slowly, "no one can help you, not even God. For here we come to the real heart of the addiction problem. Once you're clean, once you're physically detoxified, it's no longer a question of saying 'I can't.' Because here 'can't' really means 'won't.' The problem is no longer physical; it's mental. Since your physical system doesn't need it now, it's untrue and insincere to weep and cry that you can't stay off drugs. You're just saying you *won't* stay off."

The sandy-haired ex-pro shook his head sadly. "I know all that, Father," he said, "but as I've said here before, I'd be lyin' if I said I didn't want to use heroin. Man, I *love* it. It's *crazy.*"

"Yeah, I know," the priest replied. "But you also wish you could live like a square, or you wouldn't be here tonight. You want to do all the things squares do, like go to movies on Saturday nights. You don't want to be a punk any more. You want to walk on the street and look a cop straight in the eye. Because, man, *that's* what's crazy. That's what's *living*."

"It ain't easy," the ex-pro muttered.

Father Egan snorted. "Easy! So what's easy? Is it easy now, walking around like a slob without a dime in your pocket, ducking every time you see a patrol car?"

He lashed at them with his words, his eloquence finding strength. He assured them it was foolish to beg for miracles, and to realize that even if they prayed for God's help, God still only helped those who helped themselves.

"You put that needle in your arm," he warned, "and God is *not* going to pull it out for you."

His tone softened and he conceded that it was no simple feat for an addict to predict with any degree of certainty that he or she would never use drugs again. No one could plan that far ahead. "So do it the easy way," he urged, "the way that's kept hundreds of addicts off drugs for years. Make up your mind to stay off one day at a time."

He motioned to the impassive woman at the table. "Rae here was an addict for nearly twenty years. She was busted so many times she stopped counting. But I like the way she answers when I ask her how things are going. She looks at her-watch and says, 'I don't know about tomorrow, and I'm not worried about it. I'm fine right now.' She just knows she's not going to take a fix tonight. Man, she's been saying that for over thirteen years now. And it's kept her clean for thirteen years. Just imagine that. And it's that simple. When she left prison thirteen years ago—in those days when junk was real strong and kicking was real kicking—man, she decided to live just one day at a time. She didn't say 'for thirteen years' or 'for life.' It was just for today. And she's still doing it a day at a time. Always remember that today is the tomorrow you worried about yesterday. If you add up all the yesterdays in your life they only equal today. And if you subtract all the tomorrows in your life, they would only equal today, too."

He told of a recent meeting with nine ex-addicts. All were clean and working. Each had found in the "one-day-at-a-time" formula the answers and help they had never found in prison, or hospital withdrawal or psychotherapy. None were sure they would not take a fix the next day. But all were sure they would not do so that night. They had been crossing off the days on their calendars and before they realized it they had their first clean Christmas in years. Ordinary square days, unafraid of the law. Some people hadn't believed them. But *they* knew.

"So don't say you *can't* do it. There's nothing you can't do if you want it badly enough. But you've got to have a motive for wanting it. You've got to want to stay clean for your own sake as well as to please anybody else. That's just plain, human self-preservation. If staying off drugs means giving up your wife and children, still stay off drugs. You should want your own health and happiness so much that you should be willing to do anything to attain it. But under your own steam you haven't been able to do this. That's why many a junkie prays, 'God, please help me. Help me do what I can't do myself. I know staying off drugs is best for me, and I want this with all my will. But, God, my will is weak. Help me, just for today.' Even without any set form of religion, you can all do this. And remember, God and you are a *majority*. Together you can lick this thing, you can and will stay clean, one day at a time."

Father Egan had discovered NA while browsing one day through parole literature scattered on the table outside the superintendent's office at the House of Detention. Among the booklets was one on NA and he had leafed through it curiously. In the past he had frequently addressed meetings of Alcoholics Anonymous and he admired AA's philosophy, especially for its emphasis on spiritual values and their power to overcome the compulsion to drink.

Although initially struck with the similarity between an NA and an AA meeting, Father Egan soon observed an important difference between the problems facing the two organizations. Addicts who managed to abstain from drugs over an extended period and who began to re-enter normal society almost always broke contact with NA and other addicts. Having escaped a criminal environment their principal desire was not to be associated with it again in any way. On the other hand AA enjoyed the open and powerful support of many prominent people who frankly admitted to former alcoholism. Father Egan soon realized, bitterly, that there was apparently no one among the ex-addict population who was prepared to do the same. What successful man or woman would publicly declare he or she was a former drug addict, with numerous jail sentences in the past for theft or prostitution?

With the diligence that characterized his early studies of addiction itself, Father Egan minutely studied the NA program, attending all meetings when he was in the city.

Its philosophy appeared to contradict that of many experts who had spoken and written on drug addiction. Operating without membership lists, dues, constitution or by-laws, NA believed in treating addiction without being overly concerned with what had caused it. This struck a response in Father Egan; he had long felt that too much time and effort were being expended in jails and hospitals trying to learn if addicts had been frustrated or unloved in their childhood. It was no doubt important from a research standpoint to know the answers to these questions. But it meant little to the addict, except perhaps to give him an excuse for his own addiction. His compulsion to use drugs had begun in the cradle, an addict could reason, and thus it wasn't his fault and he was helpless to cope with it. To Father Egan, and to NA, this reasoning was dangerous. And at NA there was, instead, the continued effort to keep the addict away from drugs *now*.

But the organization had its troubles. Increasingly, addicts came to meetings not only to take part in its long-range program of abstinence, but in an immediate, desperate attempt to find help, to find a job, a place to live. It was on this *immediate* aspect of the drug problem that Father Egan had begun to concentrate his efforts. This urgency, this plight of the addict in need of tangible, material help, was dramatically demonstrated at one of the city's many "public forums" on addiction.

Father Egan accompanied Rae and a group of "clean" NA

members to the forum. Each former addict wore a white carnation as a symbol of abstinence. But the Junkie Priest soon became exasperated with the polite discussion. It bore no relationship to the brutal underworld he knew. Jumping to his feet, he began speaking without waiting for recognition from the chair. He was angry and he showed it.

"I don't know whether anyone here is concerned about it," he said sarcastically, "but New York is spending more money feeding the monkeys in Central Park Zoo than it is on a single female addict. It's easier to arouse public opinion about trees to be planted in Central Park or to set up a committee for better vitamins for elephants than to get anyone interested about this problem, and all of you know it."

"You would have to back that up with facts," a voice from the speakers' table retorted in annoyance.

"I don't need any facts," Father Egan shouted back furiously. "There are plenty of places in this state where monkeys are better cared for than these people."

He was joined by a lean and ascetic addict who stood up and addressed the meeting with equal vehemence.

"Do you know how *I* feel?" he demanded. "I feel like I'm drowning about twelve feet from the beach and a dozen guys like you are standing on the shore fighting among yourselves over how to save me. Should you save me with a boat, or with an oar? Should you throw me a life raft? Should you throw me this, throw me that? And all the while I'm drowning. I'm a sick man. I want a place to live, I want a job, and you're discussing research, discussing my biological problems, dissecting me like I'm some kind of organism. You've been discussing this stuff for years. There's nothing that hasn't been said about it, and you're still discussing it."

The meeting dissolved in confusion.

Slowly, NA had received cautious approval from state and city correction and parole offices. Narcotics officers who once prowled in the vicinity of the YMCA on Wednesday evenings were no longer to be seen. But this progress, Father Egan was convinced, could be immeasurably speeded if AA, with its aura of respectability, would give help and encouragement to NA, as a big brother to a little brother with a bigger problem. And if only the city or state would channel some funds to NA, perhaps to provide for a few rooms where addicts could meet in a comfortable and clublike atmosphere. If only there were some paid workers, if only one prominent personality would speak for NA as a former addict. . . .

With a start, Father Egan realized the evening's session was still in progress. Della, the Negro girl, enigmatic behind her sunglasses, had stepped to the table and was preparing to tell the story of her encounter and battle with drugs. Such accounts were a frequent item on the program of any NA meeting. They were considered effective therapy for both speaker and audience.

Della, tall and striking, stood with hands on hips. She smiled ruefully. Her voice was husky with the gentle intonation of the Mississippi Delta and seemed oddly foreign within the four drab walls of the YMCA classroom. When she commenced speaking her gaze was leveled at her audience. But as she continued Della appeared to become fascinated by her memories and her eyes fastened on some hypnotic spot on the room's bare wall. She spoke slowly, choosing her words with care.

"My name is Della Lee Potter an' I come from a farm near Greenville, Mississippi. I didn't have much upbringin' 'cause my mother died when I was six years old. My aunt brought me to *New* York an' I went to school in the Bronx. I got as far as the seventh grade an' then started missin' classes. I'd go down to the movies on Forty-Second Street an' I'd meet different boys and girls an' we'd go to apartments and dance and drink wine.

"One night this girl tol' me she had tried somethin' new. She said I'd like it, an' she ask me for a quarter an' gave me two little cigarettes and tol' me to iight one. So I did an' was smokin' it jus' like any other cigarette 'til she said, 'Hey, ya dumb dope, don't smoke it like *that,* you *wastin'* it.' So she took it from me and showed me how.

"I drew in real hard without lettin' the smoke go out. Then I began to feel lightweighted, like I was walkin' on clouds. I got so hongry I could eat up the whole refrigerator. So, from then on, every time I had a little cash I'd get two, three sticks every day. I started stayin' away from school more and more an' I was goin' to the movies all the time. I was high an' I'd walk on the street and everybody would look funny an' I'd bust out laughin' right there on the sidewalk.

"Then they took me to Children's Court an' I went to the trainin' school an' stayed there three years. I stayed in punishment more than I stayed in class, 'cause I was always fightin' an' tryin' to run away. I used to write home but I never got no answers. Christmas came an' no letters.

"So when I got out I stayed with a girl friend. An' I met this guy an' kep' company with him about four months 'til I found out I was pregnant. I didn't know what to do or where to go. No one to turn to. 'Cause I found out he was already married, which I didn't know in the beginnin'.

"I didn't want to get rid of the baby, which I could have. So I carried my child for the nine months. I was livin' in the Bronx in two rooms when the baby came, but I was still lonesome, no one to talk to. I ask a girl friend to come live with me, but I didn't know she was a drug addict an' when I found out it was too late. 'Cause one mornin' she woke up an' I notice she looked kinda funny in her eyes. An' she said to me, 'Gee, I sure need fifty cents.' I didn't ask her what for she needed fifty cents, I jus' gave it to her.

"She went out an' she was sweatin' when she came back. She went into the bathroom and locked the door. She stayed in there a long time, so I got worried and knocked on the door. She said, 'Wait a minute.' I said, 'What you doin' in there, you takin' a bath or somethin'?' But she said she was washin' up, an' I told her to open the door, 'cause it don't make no difference, two women in the bathroom. She still tol' me to wait, but I beat on the door an' she let me in.

"She had the belt aroun' her arm and the blood was runnin' down an' I saw the eyedropper in a glass. I ask her what she was doin', 'cause I had heard about dope, but I never seen it.

"She said, 'I didn't want to tell, but I had to take a fix.' I said, 'A fix of what?' An' she said, 'Heroin.'

"Bein' around her made me curious. I would see her settin' in a daze all the time like she didn't care about nothin' and I'd be worried with my problems. Where was I goin' to get this or that for the baby? Or clothes for myself or anythin'? I only had the relief check comin' in. An' I thought to myself, 'Gee, she act like she don't have a trouble in the world.'

" 'What you get out of that stuff?' I ask her one day.

" 'Best feelin' in the whole world,' she says. 'Once you get it you never want to quit.'

"She honestly, in her heart, didn't want to give it to me 'cause she tried to find all kinds of excuses not to. But an addict always depends on someone, an' she was dependin' on me for a place to live, so she gave me some. An' that's how I got started.

"I used to leave the baby next door and meet with fellers an' they'd give me money an' I'd buy stuff. One mornin' I woke up sweatin' an' I started vomitin'. I tol' my friend I was sick, that I had to go to the doctor.

"She said, 'I'll be your doctor, I know what's wrong. You need a shot. I didn't want you to start, but that's it.'

"So I was in that world a long time, eleven years. Now I'm ready to come out an' live the normal life. But I don't know only a few people that ain't junkies. My family says I'm nothin' an' that I'll always be nothin'. So I want to prove I can be someone decent outside of bein' a drug addict. 'Cause I ain't a junkie, I'm a drug addict. An' there's a difference. A junkie is someone who loses all interest in everythin' except drugs. They don' care about food, a home, nothin'. They'll sleep in the subway stations if that's where they fall. A drug addict keeps herself clean, money in her pocket an' a place to live.

"Now I know it's better to live the square life. You have to work, that's true. But while fast money goes fast, slow money goes slow. You live the worldly life an' you always got to be duckin' and dodgin' from the *police* because you always got to be doin' somethin' wrong. So that's my story and thanks for listenin'."

Della sat down in silence, which the scarred ex-fighter promptly broke by commenting loudly, "An' a pretty good story, too. Only I got a better one. I got on the stuff 'cause I didn't like bein' a loser. I had ninety pro fights an' I lost forty, an' that's too many. I fought everybody in the country an' I guess my brains are loose. That's why I shot my mouth off about the prayer."

He looked about him, discovered with surprise that everybody was listening to him, and continued.

"I don't even know what I'm doin' here," he offered. "I'm tryin' to kick a habit an' jus' bein' here with other junkies is makin' me think about junk. I been off a week an' for me that ain't bad. Now I'm here an' my insides is crawlin'. I feel like I got a hunk a ice in my stomach."

Gravely, Father Egan said, "Just make up your mind you won't take anything tonight. Worry about tomorrow when it gets here."

"Well, I gotta worry about more than that. My old lady is in the House of D. for hustlin'—she's a junkie too—an' I got to worry about stayin' off until she gets out in a month. If I'm shootin' when she gets out, she's gonna go back on it, and there we go again. But how'm I gonna stay clean a whole month? I ain't done that in seven years. I once figured I had it made, then the baby came an' I got excited an' had to take another shot."

The thumbnail chewer in the dark suit spoke up brightly. "Hey, that's a laugh," he said. "When my kid came that's what made me quit."

Scarface nodded gloomily. "Everyone comes up his own road," he said.

Rae agreed silently. She had come up a long road of her own. Nineteen years had been a weary journey.

It was a journey that had begun more than thirty years ago, when Rae Lopez, twelve years old, accepted a marijuana cigarette from another child on a littered tenement block. Marijuana was as common there as chewing gum but Rae inhaled with wide-eyed excitement. She experienced a heady sensation, enjoyed it, and her child's mind filled with strange fantasies. Months later she was sniffing cocaine and soon took the step to the final stage: heroin. The year was 1929.

Dark-eyed, precociously mature and stunningly attractive, Rae joined a Latin dance troupe. Dressed in white and scarlet skirt, ruffled tights and sleeves and narrow halter, she performed a smooth bolero with a lithe male partner. Of thirty-five people in the traveling show, twenty, including Rae, used heroin. Tampa was a good town and so was Miami; no shortage of heroin in either. The Midwest and South were often a wilderness, with the drug scarce and the dancers frantic. Soon Rae was tabbed in show business as a junkie; the show managers shrugged and shook their heads. Junkies were unreliable, the drug meant more than the act. They offered her bookings only where they knew the drug was always available, and Rae was through forever with that particular road.

At seventeen she was arrested for the first time. On a crowded Harlem sidewalk she waited, hopefully, for her heroin connection. Each day he drove past her in his new coupé, then wheeled around the block three times until she dabbed her face with a handkerchief, the signal that meant the fuzz was off the block. But that day, as she drew the handkerchief from her purse, the afternoon sun suddenly sparkled on a police badge. The fuzz, dressed in workman's overalls, seized her by her arm.

From that day her arrests and jail sentences began, recurring with painful repetition through the years. Once, at an exhausted stage of her journey, she was convinced she had conquered heroin. There was, therefore, no harm in merely taking a light shot for the weekend. At first there was not, and the weekend shots continued contentedly for a month. Then there was no harm, either, in a Monday shot, to start the week right. Next came the Wednesday shot, to shorten the long wait to Friday, and then the morning shot, to begin the day. Rae knew she was hooked again. As her habit grew, so did her arrest record at police headquarters.

On a West Side sidewalk she met a smiling neighbor, the young wife of a new connection.

"Hey, Rae," said the wife, "take this bag of groceries up for me, huh? I got to make another store. He's up there now."

Rae took the shopping bag and climbed the dim tenement stairs, sensing a warning flicker. As she entered the apartment the bag was wrenched from her grasp, a voice growling, "I'll take that."

The room was jammed with federal narcotic agents. Her connection, seated on the bed, looked at her miserably.

"Wow," was all Rae could say. She sat down, heavily.

An agent tipped the bag on the table, separated the packages and peered into a brown paper bag. He shook his head at Rae, like a parent admonishing a child.

"Shouldn't carry this stuff around," he said. "It's against the law. Let's go."

Rae shrugged. The arrest was a frame, a meatball rap, but you took it in your stride. As an addict, you took your chances every day.

Yet it was in the echoing fortress of the House of Detention that Rae was saved, for there she found NA. A strange, visionary ex-addict named Danny Carlsen was organizing exploratory NA meetings in the prison, holding them on Sunday afternoons. Sunday was a long and lonely day in jail, and Rae attended.

Danny Carlsen, a shy, diminutive Brooklynite, was the founder of NA. He had been an addict, as Rae had, since the age of twelve. His background was obscure. But he had apparently once been given morphine while suffering from an ear infection as a child. After his release from the hospital, the memory of the drug had taken deep root in his mind. He had pleaded with a hospital worker to obtain more morphine for him and a thirty-year association with drugs began. Once he had become violently ill through lack of the drug. Another hospital diagnosed his condition as appendicitis and operated on him.

After leaving the federal hospital in Lexington, Danny returned to New York to organize the first, groping attempt at self-help among addicts. He was befriended by a Salvation Army officer, Brigadier Dorothy Berry, who in turn became a dedicated worker among addicts.

"He tried to find a place where addicts could meet," Brigadier Berry later told Rae. "Everyone's hands went up in horror at the idea of allowing addicts to use any kind of facility. Finally he set up meetings in the House of Detention and began to hold them on Sundays. Later I got him permission to use a Salvation Army facility. Then he used the Labor Temple, and eventually got the okay from the YMCA. The Y has been wonderful ever since. Nobody would have thought the Y would have let addicts come in. But they have never said anything about money or membership. In fact they co-operate in every way they can. They even take care of the addicts' mail."

Rae recalled a thin, seemingly hopeless junkie she had once known, a Jewish youth in the Bronx. He had been a *real* junkie, she recalled. He was the kind of addict who kept shooting until nothing was left. Most addicts at least left a little over for the morning shot. . . . Now he had been astonishingly clean for more than a year. If he could do it, she could.

Shortly after making her decision, and still deeply depressed by the thought of the prison years that stretched before her, Rae was summoned to a conference room on the prison's ground floor. There she was told it had been decided she was too ill to serve any more time and that she was free.

Rae was stunned. She felt a miracle had occurred and was unable to believe it at first. Then she began to weep. Between sobs she vowed that as God had given her a chance, so she would give NA a chance.

Through NA Rae found her release from the horror and compulsion of addiction. Through persuading other addicts to join NA she found the purpose in life that perpetuated that freedom. She threw her energies into NA, continuing the work when Danny died, and was overwhelmed with emotion one year to receive two hundred and fifty Christmas cards from "clean" addicts who had attended NA meetings.

In 1961 a proud day came for Rae. The New York City Department of Health invited her to speak at a meeting on addiction. Later that year she was hired as a full-time city employee in the department's Office of Narcotics Co-ordination. Her qualifications: an unexcelled knowledge of addiction and single-minded dedication to its victims.

A tense moment had come while filling out her employment application. One form was for Police Department inspection. It contained the question: *Have you ever been arrested?* Unhesitatingly Rae wrote: *Yes. Various times. I am a former addict.*

Now a smartly dressed and vigorous woman of forty-four, Rae reflected with some satisfaction on the growth of NA. She had originated chapters in the prisons at Marquette and Jackson, Michigan, and in Passaic County, Newark, Hackensack and Hoboken, New Jersey, all by mail. Two were planned for Philadelphia and she had been invited there by the city, expenses paid. It marked the first time she had been offered public funds for any NA project. The organization operated without funds, public or otherwise, and money was a constant problem. The NA newsletter list was growing— more than five hundred names—and the last edition had cost forty dollars. In addition, she desperately wanted to visit the NA chapters she had instituted by mail, but the fare was beyond her reach.

Rae looked at Father Egan. He had walked into a meeting one night, unannounced and unexpected. For years NA had been trying to find a priest and now it had its own chaplain.

"It's gettin' late," she announced, "we better wind it up. Everyone stand up and say the Lord's Prayer."

The little group gathered in front of her table, solemnly joined hands and recited the prayer. Scarface kept his eyes on the floor and said nothing.

The junkies, the nursing students, Rae and Father Egan filed out of the room and headed across Twenty-Third Street to the Automat for their customary cup of coffee together.

"Join us?" Father Egan asked Scarface.

"Nah, I'm goin' uptown."

Father Egan nodded with understanding. He knew what this struggling youth meant by "uptown." If he wanted heroin tonight it was no use arguing with him. He would have to make his own decision.

In the Automat people glanced up curiously as the group entered.

Outside, the young ex-fighter halted at the steps leading down the Seventh Avenue subway. He smashed a fist into his palm, then turned and pushed his way through the Automat's revolving door.

8. MARIE

1

ON THE littered Harlem sidewalk, deserted and faintly menacing at 3 A.M., Marie walked, almost ran, to meet her heroin connection. Oblivious to everything but her craving for the drug, she failed to notice three shadows that flitted noiselessly behind her.

The night was warm and the street lamps' baleful glare was softened by millions of stars in the city's sky. Their glow bathed the harsh landscape below, dispersing gloom from a thousand sinister rooftops and shadowed doorways. The gentle light poured on rotting, crumbling dwellings that stretched for block upon dismal block in all directions, where life and love were pursued furtively, desperately and often cruelly in the rustling, uneasy night.

Marie, stumbling in her haste, tripping on her high heels, frantic for her fix, fingered a thick roll of bills in her hand. She ran up a flight of steps and tapped lightly on a darkened brownstone's door. The door opened an inch and a woman's voice said irritably, "Come on in, you sure are late."

On the street, the three shadows melted away.

Inside the doorway, in a barely lit corridor, a fat woman dressed in a stained housecoat and felt slippers, her hair in curlers, her eyes like slits, peered at Marie.

"Gimme the money," she demanded.

"No. Gimme the bag first," Marie countered, her eyes watering. "How's the quality?"

"Quality good," muttered the fat woman as she handed Marie a small white package from inside her housecoat.

"What's the count?"

"Count good."

The words were an old junkie dialogue. Marie always liked to know, even in moments of her most desperate desire for drugs, how far the heroin had been diluted or cut with milk sugar. The less dilution, the better the quality, the better the count, i. e., the ratio of heroin to milk sugar.

The connection pushed a five-dollar bill down into the housecoat and shuffled off into the corridor's gloom. Marie heard the felt slippers pad up the stairs until a door slammed. In the creaking silence of the ancient rooming house she hurried into a hallway toilet, and amid stench and filth drew a battered syringe from her underclothing and eased her torment with a full and satisfying injection of heroin.

Marie leaned against the peeling corridor wall for a long time, breathing deeply, then opened the front door and emerged into the street. She smiled foolishly at the beauty of the starlit night and walked slowly in the direction of her tiny, cluttered room three blocks distant.

She hummed softly, her head nodding. As she neared her doorway, lined with brimming garbage cans, a light step fell behind her. An arm wound about her neck, snapping her head back agonizingly, and a hand clamped over her mouth. She was dragged, rigid with terror, into the building's pitch-dark storage basement. Eyes wide, Marie heard the muffled voices of three men around her.

"Let's have the bread," a voice rasped, and the hand was released from her mouth.

"What bread, man?" she wailed. "What you want with me?"

The blow struck her full in the face, stunning her. Dazed and choking she fumbled inside her dress and handed her attacker, a vague shape in the darkness, the roll of bills.

"How much here?" he grated.

"Ninety-five an' that's all."

"Where's the rest?"

"Ain't no rest. I had a hundred 'til I copped jus' now for five bucks."

Again the fist slammed into her face. Marie groaned, pleading with the man not to hit her again.

"You got more'n a hundred for them furs," he said. "Give!"

In a haze, Marie wondered how he knew about the big theft she had committed earlier in the day, then recoiled under a rain of blows. Hands ripped her clothing in a search for money. Then she lay there, exhausted and unprotesting, as the trio raped her. Finally, in a scuffle of shoes, she heard them leave.

Marie remained still until she felt strength flow back into her body. She crawled slowly and painfully from the basement and reached the sidewalk. There, as she staggered like a wounded animal toward her doorway, a patrol car's spotlight jabbed the darkness, blinding her.

Marie fainted.

Three hours later she woke up in Bellevue Hospital to find Father Egan staring at her. She gazed around her, realized her head was splitting with pain, then nodded to him without surprise, familiarly and miserably. Tears of self-pity rolled down her ebony face.

"Here I is, Father," she moaned. "In trouble again."

Father Egan shook his head. He had known Marie for two years, ever since she called him one night and lied that she had just been released from Lexington and needed money to find a place to live. He had given her enough for a week's rent and she had promptly spent it on heroin. When he found out about it the next day he shrugged. Her lie was nothing; he gave her another week's rent, but this time accompanied her to the rooming house and saw that she paid for the week in advance. Since then she had become one of his regulars, and he met her coming and going as she traveled in and out of the House of Detention. Marie had to steal, he knew, to sustain her ferocious heroin habit. And most of the time, with her startling skill at shoplifting, she managed fairly well.

A nurse had called him with the news that Marie was in Bellevue and he had driven to the hospital immediately. He looked pityingly at her thin face, framed by heavy bandage dressings, and asked what had happened this time.

"They must have known about my big sting, Father," she said, shaking her head.

"What big sting?"

"I made a big steal, Father. Over in Jersey. Somethin' that needed a cool, light touch. Which is what I got."

"Which is why you're here. But go on."

"I heard about it from a junkie who came to visit me from Newark, Father. He said there was a little fur store there jus' waitin' to be hit. So I hit it."

Marie told Father Egan how her ears had virtually quivered at the suggestion that she rob the store. It was easy, she was told. Nobody but an old man who owned the place worked there. She had boarded a train for Newark thirty minutes later and discovered it was just as she had been told: a small shop on a side street.

"Father, I pushed the door open, an' the first thing I notice is that no bell rang. Get it? Then I see no one in the front, jus' an old man in the workroom in the back. I look around, and *man!* On the rack was wraps, coats and stoles, all kinds."

Within seconds two mink stoles were securely and snugly gripped between her legs, hidden under a full skirt specially worn for the occasion.

"Then, as I went out—the doorbell rang. I *froze*, Father. The old man came outa the back room and I pretended I was comin' in the door instead of goin' out. So I stand there for fifteen minutes, with his minks between my knees, while I talk about buyin' a fur coat. Finally I walk out of there and make it back to the city okay. An' all I get from the fence was a lousy hundred bucks. He'll get two-fifty apiece for them. But the word must have got around fast, for those three monkeys were waitin' for me after I got my fix from you know where."

She began to cry and Father Egan looked at her with mild astonishment. In the two years he had known this hard little jungle product he had never seen her cry. He placed a pack of cigarettes on her bedside table and promised to return the next day.

Marie sighed as she watched him leave, walking with his jaunty, almost nautical gait. She felt depressed and decided she didn't even want a fix. It just wasn't worth it any more, she lectured herself. All her scheming, her time in jails— she was twenty-four and had spent a total of three years in prisons—the beatings, the hiding from the law, the desperation for drugs, had got her nowhere. And there was no end in sight except more of the same. She turned her head on her pillow and wept again.

Maríe, born in the desperate world of East Harlem, had been a thief, a highly skilled shoplifter or booster, for five years. She had been arrested four times. She had stolen thousands of items from stores throughout the New York area and had supported a heroin habit often costing fifty dollars a day.

She had not been born with her talent for theft. She had, in fact, paid to acquire it. She had attended boosting school.

As a beginning student, at the age of nineteen, Marie entered department stores with a group of skilled thieves to observe their techniques. Initially, she did nothing except deliberately act in a suspicious manner. This diverted the attention of store detectives and sales personnel from her companions who were methodically looting the counters. But Marie carefully watched how the professionals, moving with lightning speed, could roll dresses into tight, neat bundles, slip them under their skirts and between their legs, then walk away with a seemingly natural stride.

Some women, she learned, wore special voluminous bloomers—or boosting drawers, as they were called—on shoplifting expeditions. Still others wore two pairs of these cavernous garments. In fact winter was the best shoplifting season; you wore more clothes.

Gradually Marie felt more and more confident that she could equal her instructor's dexterity. The professionals were anxious for her to try. Any proceeds she earned while still under their instruction would be shared equally with them, as tuition fees.

One day, nervous but determined, Marie accompanied a coldly professional youth to a crowded midtown department store. They carefully selected an hour near closing time when salesgirls were tired and relatively unobservant. The tutor, sharp-eyed, told Marie she would make her "solo flight" that day, adding judiciously that the fastest and most effective way to acquire confidence was actually to steal an item and walk out of the store.

He inspected a rack of spring dresses, in a medium price range. These would do, he said. In a blur of movement, he seized one from the rack, rolled it into a neat, tight bundle and handed it to Marie. There was no time to think; the dress felt like a grenade in her hand. She snatched it from him and swept it between her knees.

"Now walk," he commanded. "Or go to jail."

Marie walked, terrified. She relaxed only when the dress was safely in her shopping bag outside.

But she was determined to operate alone at the first opportunity. To be completely sure of herself she continued under supervision for several more weeks, until she knew she could stand directly before a salesgirl, engage her in conversation and deftly filch an item at the same time.

Marie remained in Bellevue for several days, her heroin addiction mildly assuaged by pain-killing sedatives. Father Egan came to visit her often and on the day before her release he asked her what she intended to do when she got out.

"Going back to boosting and drugs, Marie?"

"Don't know nothin' else, Father."

"Do you want to stop?"

Marie sighed and shrugged her ebony shoulders helplessly.

"Sure, Father. I always want to stop. But you know how I am."

"Will you give Lexington a try?"

She thought for a moment and shrugged again. Why not?

"Yeah, I guess so," she said hesitantly. "Whatever you say, Father."

"Good, Marie. I'll come back this afternoon and tell you what to do."

Father Egan had paid a visit to the famed United States Public Health Service hospital at Lexington after hearing continuous talk about "K-Y" from his addicts. He had found a meticulously maintained structure, deep in the celebrated blue grass country of Kentucky. It was true a certain prison-like atmosphere prevailed there, but it was at a refreshing minimum after the House of Detention and other jails he knew. One doctor, in fact, had described the institution as "more like a prison than most hospitals and more like a hospital than most prisons."

In the summer evening he spent there, Father Egan observed the relaxed attitude of the inmates, lounging and strolling in the open air. None of the trappings of a jail were present: no watchtowers, no guns. Not even those who had been sent to the hospital as federal prisoners wore a prison uniform.

Inside, rooms were large and airy and there was a sympathetic and tolerant attitude on the part of the staff toward the addict inmates. There was, however, a somewhat fatalistic aspect to this kindness, as if the staff accepted the fact that most patients who left the hospital would soon return.

This disturbed him slightly. It was one thing to expect an addict to become readdicted and to return, but another to reveal it. He knew, from his own experience, that mere glances and remarks could condition an addict to view himself as a hopeless case. In addition, he remonstrated mildly with the hospital's staff about some extreme pornography he saw pasted on the walls of the men's quarters. Such displays, he argued, were not exactly the best therapy for the breaking of a narcotic habit. He was assured that more inspections of the quarters would be carried out.

Father Egan had returned to New York by train, in the company of two young male addicts. On the long night journey the three men soon fell asleep.

As early light brightened the countryside speeding by, he awoke to see one of the addicts staring quietly before him. The man smiled when Father Egan greeted him and said, unexpectedly and thoughtfully, "Father, give me one good reason to stay off drugs, and I'll stay off."

There was the heart of it, the priest thought. Unless an addict had that reason, all the preaching, all the sermons, all the scientific treatment in the world, would not help him. He chatted softly with the addict for a while until they both dozed off to the rhythm of the train's wheels.

Now he considered Marie. Did she have a reason to stay off drugs? Only Marie knew. There was no doubt, though, that she needed more medical care, of the type only Lexington could provide.

Father Egan's meeting with Commissioner Anslinger, now so long ago, had paid off handsomely. Often, when he had a case he considered demanding immediate attention, he could pull strings quietly and effectively. Marie, he knew, was undoubtedly such a case. If she were not sent to Lexington, or anywhere out of the city, the only alternative was to see her return immediately to drugs and theft. Father Egan placed his usual call to Washington.

Within hours Lexington officials were telephoning back to Bellevue to say a bed was ready for Marie. She would not have to make the customary written application for admission; this had already been approved. They advised, however, that she be provided with some medication to take with her on the twenty-one-hour bus ride from New York to Kentucky.

Marie was accordingly given a small package containing six methadone pills. These, it was calculated, would be adequate to cope with any withdrawal symptoms that might arise during her journey. She fingered the package as if it contained priceless jewelry.

When she was dressed and ready to leave Bellevue, Father Egan handed her two letters.

"One is from Bellevue and one is from me," he told her. "They're addressed to the medical officer-in-charge at Lexington, testifying that you've been a patient at Bellevue, that you've been detoxified but that you need more treatment to help you beat your habit."

Marie thanked him dumbly. She felt past caring, and was only too happy and too grateful to place herself completely in the hands of someone like Father Egan. She had never been to Lexington, yet was strangely incurious about what lay ahead of her. Somehow everything would be all right, and if it was not, nothing was lost.

Father Egan handed her a ten-dollar bill. "Use it for meals on the trip," he said, "and nothing else." He reminded her to save three dollars for the taxi ride from Lexington bus station to the hospital, six miles west of the city on the Leestown Pike. No public transportation would be available for that portion of her journey.

The immediate problem was to transport Marie from Bellevue, on the east side of Manhattan, to the bus station, on the west side. He could not risk letting her make even that short journey alone, not with ten dollars in her pocket. A mountain of heroin lay in the labyrinth between First and Eighth

Avenues, an obstacle Marie could almost certainly not cross alone. He therefore took her gently by the arm and led her to his car in the hospital's parking lot. On the drive across town, he stopped only to buy her a pair of shoes and some clothing.

Marie felt desperately alone as she boarded the bus, yet at the same time subdued and calm. Through the raised window she said to Father Egan, "I hope this is it, Father. I sure hope I'm ready."

He assured her she was, and prayed silently for her. The bus rolled out of the driveway and she was gone.

2

The bus swept through the Holland Tunnel and emerged in sunlight in New Jersey. Marie gazed across the Hudson River at the vast stone pile of Manhattan, its peaks jagged against the pure sky. Then, with a curve of the highway, the city disappeared from view.

On the New Jersey Turnpike, stretching ahead in the afternoon haze, the hours passed swiftly for Marie. A vague anticipation of clean white sheets, doctors and nurses filled her with satisfaction. That will be nice, she told herself, if only for a while. How come that Father Egan so good to me? She shrugged and gazed idly at the Jersey farmland.

The bus thundered into gathering darkness and Marie relaxed as tension slowly ebbed from her body. Gradually she dozed, to awake suddenly and fearfully as the bus came to a halt. It was dark and she peered from her window to see the bus had stopped in the main street of a small town. And over a corner pharmacy a green neon light flashed on and off in terrifying succession:

DRUGS—DRUGS—DRUGS—DRUGS—

Marie swallowed hard. She tried to tear her gaze from the flashing, malevolent sign but was hypnotized by it. As she stared, her eyes round with fascination, a tiny, icy trickle entered her stomach.

In desperation Marie tried to ignore the insidious sensation which she bitterly recognized as the first, subtle intimation that the desire for heroin was about to sweep through her body. But the trickle seemed to grow into a probing finger that curled gently but insistently into her entrails. Perspiration sprang to her face as the bus jolted into motion once again. The sign vanished.

Marie leaned back in her seat, breathing hard. The craving for the needle and its blessed escape suddenly smashed at her brain and she groped frantically for her purse and the precious pills it contained.

She sat bolt upright. The purse was open on the empty seat beside her, its contents scattered. Feverishly, by the dim pencil light above her, she searched for the small package. It was gone.

Biting her lip, Marie peered through the gloom at her fellow passengers. She did not know how long she had been asleep but felt it had been several hours. One of the passengers was almost certainly a junkie, had recognized her as such, and had stolen the pills. . . .

There was nothing she could do. As iciness spread through her body she huddled into the corner of her seat for warmth and prepared for the ordeal to come. Within an hour she felt nauseated; her nose was running, her muscles twitched, gooseflesh crept over her skin and her eyes burned. The beginnings of pain settled in her joints and she sank her head to her chest and wrapped her arms tightly about her shoulders.

After what seemed to be hours of traveling through a black and endless void, Marie became dimly aware that the bus was entering a large city. She spotted its name on a highway marker; it was a well-known industrial center. In the first light of dawn she saw large factories, their chimneys gaunt against the sky, passing by on either side.

As the bus neared the midtown area, Marie felt she was approaching insanity. She would have to get off; anything was better than enduring her present suffering and the greater torment that lay ahead.

When the bus halted, Marie hurried to the door clutching her small suitcase and was the first passenger to leave. She stood alone and hesitant on the bus ramp, then entered the

almost empty waiting room. A clock above her pointed to
5 A.M.

Marie found a coin telephone, fumbled for a dime, and
told the operator, "I want to call New York collect, for a
Father Daniel Egan." She gave the number.

Within seconds she heard Father Egan's voice, and tears
came to her eyes as she told him where she was and that
her pills had been stolen. After a moment's hesitation, Father Egan spoke to her slowly and clearly.

"Listen to me carefully, Marie," he said. "Follow my instructions. Don't panic. You have some money, right? Now
take a taxi to the nearest hospital, any hospital. Remember
you're a sick person, that you're not hiding from the police.
Go in just like anybody else. Go to the emergency room
and show them the two letters I gave you. Just ask the doctor
or the nurse there for one methadone pill or anything equiva-
lent. Tell them you just want something to sustain you until
you get to Lexington, which is about four or five hours from
where you are now. Okay?"

"Okay, Father, I'll do it."

"Call me or write me to let me know what happened."

Marie softly replaced the receiver and hailed a taxi outside. Pain was penetrating the remotest corners of her body
now. She croaked at the driver to hurry to the nearest hospital, explaining that she had suddenly become ill.

Minutes later the taxi swept into a curving driveway and
halted at an emergency room entrance.

Marie paid the driver and climbed out stiffly. She pushed
open a pair of swing doors and walked into a silent corridor.
A nurse looked up inquiringly from her desk.

"Good morning," she said brightly. "Can I help you?"

Fumblingly, Marie produced the letters Father Egan had
given her and handed them to the nurse, who looked at them
in puzzlement.

"Y'see," Marie said hoarsely, "I'm jes' on my way to the
hospital down at Lexington, but someone done stole my pills
an' Father Egan—he's in New York—he told me to come
here an' jus' pick up one more to get me there okay. 'Cause
I'm real sick right now without one."

The nurse frowned. She inspected the letters again and shook her head.

"You mean you want us to give you a, er, a pill? You're a drug addict?"

Marie nodded and managed a wan smile. The brightness vanished, however, from the nurse's voice. She told Marie to sit down and disappeared through a nearby door. A few seconds later a man's head poked out of the door. He looked at Marie, nodded, then withdrew. The nurse came out and sat behind her desk again. She did not look at Marie.

Marie waited, and nothing happened. She tried to catch the nurse's eye. But for some reason the unsmiling face framed by the neat white cap seemed to be studiously avoiding her.

Suddenly Marie heard an automobile skid to a halt in the driveway outside. The car's doors slammed, the swing doors to the corridor opened and two uniformed police officers strode into the hospital. They were young and husky and their heavy pistols slapped against their thighs as they walked.

Marie, perspiration beaded on her forehead, stared at them vacantly.

The officers approached the desk. One of them jerked a thumb at Marie. "This her?" he asked.

The nurse nodded silently.

The officer grabbed Marie's arm and pulled her to her feet. "Okay," he said. "Let's go."

Marie shook her head. Panic seized her.

"No, no," she cried. "I ain't done nothin'. Why you pickin' me up? What fo'?"

"Come on!" shouted the patrolman. "I said let's go!"

His grip tightened painfully on Marie's thin arm and he dragged her with him toward the doors. As the other officer held the doors open, Marie managed a single glance back at the nurse. She sat with head down, staring at her desk.

Marie was placed in the back seat of the patrol car. The officer who had seized her climbed in beside her. The other patrolman took the wheel. The car glided smoothly out of the hospital driveway and into city traffic. Marie covered her face with her hands and wept.

The police car rolled into another driveway and halted in the rear of a large modern building. With her elbow firmly grasped in the officer's large hand, Marie was ushered into an elevator then down an immaculate, tiled corridor. One of the officers rapped smartly on a door bearing a sign, DETECTIVE DIVISION, then pushed her inside. She stood, her head drooping in misery, before a lean plainclothes officer seated behind a desk.

"Got us a little New York junkie, lieutenant," said one of the uniformed officers. "She was trying to pick up some pills or somethin' at the hospital. They called us."

The lieutenant looked at her coldly. Marie dropped her eyes. Her body was ice-cold and the old, familiar knotted pains were settling into her knees, elbows, stomach and behind her eyes. She cried quietly, in short, choking sobs.

"Cut that out," said the lieutenant. "No one's gonna hurt you. You just got to learn that we don't want any New York dopeheads in this town. If you were on your way to Lex you should have kept goin'. Anyway, we'll just lock you up and check you out and if you're okay you can take a bus down to Lex tomorrow."

He nodded and the two uniformed officers led Marie to another room. She was photographed and fingerprinted. Her name, age and place of birth were typed on a small white card. No one seemed concerned that she appeared to be ill. Next, Marie was taken to the women's floor of the city jail and placed in a small, heavily barred cell.

She threw herself on the narrow cot and gave herself up to the torment that engulfed her. During the day and throughout the following night she vomited constantly and developed violent diarrhea. When her cell door was opened, some twenty-four hours after she was led in, she was an exhausted, trembling wreck.

Back in the lieutenant's office Marie was told that her record had been checked and that she was free to leave. A clerk returned her purse and the letters she had presented at the hospital.

"And keep going," said the detective. "If we see you here again, we'll run you in again."

Somehow, in a daze of pain and weariness, Marie found

the bus station. A few hours later she arrived at the hospital. She produced her letters and was immediately admitted. After her suitcase and her person had been searched for drugs she was physically examined and placed in the hospital's Withdrawal Ward.

The following day she was able to write to Father Egan. She told him everything that had happened.

Father Egan read the letter three times, the flush on his face deepening each time. Finally he crumpled the letter into a tight ball and hurled it from him in his anger.

3

At Lexington Marie was immediately plunged into a scientific program designed to achieve a single but ambitious goal—to return her to society free of physical and mental dependence on drugs. It is a program based on two decades of experience and research.

The hospital, sprawling over a one-thousand-acre tract, opened on the sunny Saturday afternoon of May 25, 1935. At the ceremony, Assistant Surgeon General Walter Treadway observed:

"The dedication and opening of this institution represent a change in the policy of the United States toward the so-called drug problem. This is an expression on the part of the government that restrictive laws governing commerce in narcotics are not the only measure to be applied to the possible solution of the medico-social problems of drug addiction. The isolation and segregation of drug addicts and the objective of medical treatment appear likely and necessary. Their presence and contact with other individuals in American communities are a potential danger and a causative factor in the production of further addiction."

Many of Mr. Treadway's thoughts were found to be as valid almost thirty years later as the day he voiced them, although some differences of opinion—especially on hospital segregation of addicts—later developed in the medical profession. But the day marked a major advance for those contending that addiction is primarily a medical and social problem, not a criminal one.

After six years, the first female patients were admitted to the hospital, arriving by transfer from the Federal Reformatory for Women at Alderson, West Virginia.

When Marie was admitted, sixteen years later, the hospital was functioning under carefully and rigidly designed federal rules.

As far as the hospital is concerned an addict is anyone who uses a habit-forming narcotic drug to the point of endangering the public morals, health, safety or welfare and who has lost the power of self-control.

Federal law uses the term "narcotic drugs" to cover a wide range of products—heroin, cocaine, marijuana, opium, morphine, methadone, paregoric, peyote "and any other drug, the sale of which may by executive order and/or Presidental proclamation be covered under the Harrison Narcotic Act."

At Lexington, records of admission, treatment and discharge of voluntary patients, such as Marie, are confidential. The hospital provides and launders patients' clothing and permits the entry of such personally owned toilet articles as combs, brushes and razors. But beauty aids, lotions, lipsticks and facial creams—easy hiding places for drugs—are forbidden. Anyone caught trying to bring narcotics into the hospital is subject to federal prosecution.

But Marie found a pleasant atmosphere at Lexington. In her first letter to Father Egan she wrote:

> I have as nice a little room as I've ever lived in during my life. There are drapes on the windows and the floors are waxed until they shine. And we can keep a radio on all night long if we wish. There's a nice laundry and a washateria, and a beauty parlor. And the commissary is just like walking into a supermarket at home.

Her medical treatment was essentially simple. She was given methadone as a mild narcotic to help taper off her dependence on heroin. Gradually the doses of methadone were lessened until her body no longer needed them. Her acute desire for drugs vanished after about two weeks and this was followed by a further two-week period of convalescence. She regained much of her strength, weight and appetite, but still experienced some restlessness and irritability and had difficulty in sleeping.

Dr. James Lowry, a former medical officer-in-charge at Lexington, has written that recovery of the body from physical dependence on drugs usually takes about four months. He noted that this differs from patient to patient, depending on the size of the habit and on the patient's physical condition.

For Marie, the process took a little more than three months. She was then discharged from the Withdrawal Ward and placed in the Orientation Ward. In a letter to Father Egan from Orientation she wrote:

> This is what we call Skid Row. But it's pretty nice and they give us all kinds of interviews. You know, psychology. Some tests are with ink blots, and there is addition and subtraction, to find out what your mentality is like. And they asked me how many times I had been arrested, if I had any kids, if I was married. It's interesting, you know.

Actually Marie was subjected to a highly scientific series of tests and interviews by the hospital's vocational, social, correctional and psychiatric specialists. Results of these were evaluated by a physician assigned to her case, who in turn planned a program considered to have the best chance of returning her to society free of drug dependence. A vocational supervisor reported regularly to Marie's doctor on her attitude to tasks allotted her.

Marie worked in Lexington's mail room. All mail leaving and entering the institution is censored. It was Marie's job to open packages for the inspection of a federal employee in charge. She enjoyed the work and although she talked incessantly about drugs and boosting with other girls, she wrote Father Egan that she felt no physical or mental need for narcotics.

I listen to music all the time or I crochet a little. They come and go; a bell wakes us up, another bell rings for breakfast. Of course you can fix coffee in your room if you want to, but I go in to breakfast. There's French toast and bacon, cereal, eggs and all the milk and coffee you want. You can always go back for more if you're still hungry.

As a voluntary patient Marie could leave the hospital at any time. But she deliberately remained there a full six months, until certain that she would not let Father Egan down when she returned to New York. She knew the number of actual cures achieved by Lexington was low, but she was determined to be among them.

The federal government maintains one other hospital similar to Lexington's, at Fort Worth, Texas. Only the Lexington hospital admits women. And some 40 percent of those who have passed through both hospitals have made the journey once before. They are classified as "repeaters." No exact statistics are available, but it is estimated that more than half of those treated at Lexington and Fort Worth return to drugs. Yet upon discharge from the hospitals they are as physically free of dependence on drugs as available science can make them.

Eventually Marie was able to write an excited letter to Father Egan:

I have good news. I was called to our Ward doctor's office and he gave me a MHB [maximum hospital benefit], which means I'm okay to leave here. So I'll be getting out in two weeks. I'll write and let you know what time. I don't know whether I can get some money for transportation, but maybe I can borrow some here. I will go to see the social worker about it. I don't have money or ticket yet.

You will have no more problems with me. I don't have any more desire for drugs. All I need is a start when I get back. You can check this with the doctor here.

Now I really don't want to go home by bus because of

my experience in that town on the way here. There is a stopover there and they have my photograph and finger-prints and I don't want a repeat performance. So I'll try to come by train. Please pray for me so that everything will be all right.

Being healthy and normal feels so precious. I will never be sorry you sent me here. This is the best hospital in the world. Well, Father Egan, duty calls. I have to go back to work now. God bless you for all you have done for me. There are a few girls here who know you and send regards.

Respectfully,
MARIE

When Father Egan received the letter he did exactly what Marie had asked; he prayed for her.

If only there was somewhere where he could care for Marie after she stepped off that train, he thought, if only there was a halfway house in New York. As an admirer of Lexington and its treatment programs, he was also one of the hospital's severest critics. But it was a wholly construc-tive criticism, leveled against a situation over which the hospital's staff had no control. What happened to the addict after she left the hospital, whom she met, where she went, what she did, was beyond the reach of that staff, despite their months of care.

Yet often he wondered what the state of knowledge of the addiction problem would be if Lexington had not come into being. As a laboratory for firsthand study of the prob-lem it was unsurpassed. He wished, in fact, that some who were regarded as experts in the addiction field would tap the enormous reservoir of information accumulated at Lex-ington during its almost thirty years of existence. Too often he encountered so-called authorities on narcotics enthused with new ideas on the subject. Sometimes they were given grants and stipends to conduct further studies into their in-novations only to learn that Lexington had made identical discoveries years before. There ought to be a centralized pool of information on which anyone interested in drug ad-diction could draw, he thought.

When Marie returned to New York he felt guardedly optimistic about her. She had gained weight and though she looked small and alone in vast, crowded Pennsylvania Station she smiled widely when she saw him. They walked from the building laughing together. He told her a hotel room was ready for her and that the next step was to find her a job. Marie nodded hopefully.

Father Egan drove her to the hotel and gave her a week's rent in advance. He instructed her to call him the following morning.

The call did not come. He telephoned the hotel and the clerk told him Marie had left hurriedly during the night, leaving her suitcase and belongings in her room. She had not been seen since. Father Egan's heart sank.

Two days later he walked briskly and routinely into the House of Detention. Marie sat on a corridor bench with a group of new arrivals.

"Marie!" Father Egan almost shouted. "What are you doing here? You just got back to town!"

Marie smiled cheerfully and shrugged.

"Father, I just couldn't help it. I slipped again. I only paid for one night's rent in the hotel. And when I went up to that room an' sat there alone for twenty minutes somethin' inside me gave way. I got that old icy feelin' in my stomach an' I knew I couldn't fight it. I tried an' tried for more than an hour, Father. But I ended up runnin' out of there and goin' uptown to get a fix. Don't ask me why, I just don't know. I spent all my money on heroin an' I just couldn't face you an' ask you for more money. So I tried boostin' again to get some more money for the week's rent. I was caught on the first try an' here I am."

Father Egan fought back his exasperation. He asked her, "So what are you smiling about, Marie? I would have thought you'd be crying."

The smile disappeared from the girl's face. She looked at him steadily. "Father," she said. "I jus' ain't got no more tears left."

His exasperation instantly turned to compassion. "Sure, Marie," he said softly. "I know. I'll try to get you paroled in my care and, as long as you're back on drugs again, I'll also try to get you into the hospital."

"Whatever you say, Father."

At the hospital he had in mind, a severe building on an old and weary Lower East Side thoroughfare, she would at least have another chance. Perhaps he could reach her there in another way. For it was there that he offered Mass with the strangest of the city's congregations.

9. THE CURE

1

AT THE DOOR of each ward he stopped and called out: "Get up, girls! Wake up! I'll be back in an hour! Get ready!"

The replies came in sleepy women's voices.

"What time is it, anyway?"

"Is it cold outside?"

"Father, I cussed out the nurse last night."

Dressed in his brown, ankle-length friar's robe, with white cord about his waist and sandals on his feet, Father Egan pushed a rubber-wheeled wagon along the hospital corridor.

On the wagon were loaded his portable altar—a handy affair with collapsible legs—his chalice, vestments, candles and flowers. The altar's gold-embroidered draperies had been painstakingly stitched by drug addicts in the cells of the House of Detention for Women.

He trundled the hospital wagon to the end of the brightly lit corridor. A nurse led him through two locked doors into another section of the floor. She locked the doors behind him. Now he was in the men's section of the drug wards. He stopped at a nurses' station and pressed a button activating the public address system.

His voice crackled loudly over the speaker. "Good morning, men. This is Father Egan speaking. We'll have Sunday

Mass, men, Sunday services in fifteen minutes in the TV room. That's fifteen minutes, men. Everyone's invited. Remember, men, this is the time to pray. Not when you're in the street and sick, not when you're in a panic for junk, not when you're busted in jail, but now, men."

The speaker clicked off and Father Egan continued through the corridor pushing the wagon before him. He entered the floor's recreation room and busily went to work. When the first of his congregation arrived the small, drab room had been neatly transformed into a chapel. The portable altar had been set up in much the same manner as an army chaplain's in the field. The Mass book, candles, wine, water and flowers were arranged between statues of Saint Martin de Porres, the Negro Saint, and Saint Jude, the Saint of the Impossible.

The addicts shuffled in, scratching their morning beards and clutching their faded robes about them. They were the city's junkies, the habitués of its jails, the sweepings of its concrete-covered earth. In the morning, in shapeless hospital clothes, with tattoo- and needle-marked arms, tired eyes and stubbed chins, they appeared even more forlorn than usual.

"Just be as reverent as you can, men," Father Egan said quietly.

As the Mass progressed he was conscious once more of the unusual nature of his parish. Occasionally it was difficult to synchronize services with the hospital's medication schedules. If any of the worshipers here had just received their morning dose of methadone, for example, they might be in too drugged a condition to derive much benefit from the service. Some of them were, in fact, nodding quite sleepily. God in a cave, he thought, now God in a TV room. It was an exclusive parish indeed.

At the end of the service the addicts helped him load his altar and the other items back on the hospital wagon. They watched until he disappeared through the double locked doors into the women's section. Then they returned slowly to their beds.

Father Egan shoved the wagon into the women's recreation room. He pushed the ping-pong table and a few chairs aside and once more set up his chapel. By the time the first girls entered the room the vigil lights were burning and he was ready. The girls came in, singly and in groups, until about twenty were seated around him. They were dressed in pink hospital robes and gowns. Some padded on bedroom slippers, some had their hair in curlers, some yawned continuously. Others reserved this one occasion of the week to dress in neat, self-made clothes, to do their hair and apply subdued makeup.

"Good morning, girls," he called cheerfully.

"Good morning, Father Egan," came the chorused reply.

On one of his first Sunday mornings at the hospital he had recalled, with sudden and vivid clarity, the story of Father Damien, the leper. Father Damien was one of the first priests to live at the leper colony of Molokai, one of the Hawaiian islands. Toward the end of his life he had contracted leprosy and one day, in a moving sermon, he found himself using the word "we" instead of "you" when addressing the lepers before him. He said "we lepers," and never again "you lepers." No one had known of his leprosy until that day.

At first unconsciously, the word "we" had similarly crept into Father Egan's own sermons. He had never taken a fix, never stuck a needle in his arm, and had no desire or need to. But he had so identified himself with his addicts that using "we" seemed more appropriate than "you." And it certainly was one way, he reasoned, in which he could place himself more firmly on the addicts' side of the fence, where he could not preach *at* them. After all, their problems, frustrations and agonies were equally his.

When it came time for the sermon his message was simple and direct.

"Girls," he began crisply, "all of us addicts here have one thing in common—we want to be happy. The search for happiness is the key to all our problems."

The faces before him reflected varying degrees of comprehension and emotion. Some were bitter and withdrawn, as if fearful of dropping an instinctive guard; some seemed eager and marked by confused, tragic yearnings. Others were vacant and slack-jawed, still others inscrutable.

Father Egan continued, his voice clear and slightly impassioned. "But unfortunately, girls, years ago we made the mistake of confusing thrills with happiness. Thrills, girls, are in the body. Happiness is in the soul. Thrills, girls, are on the surface. Happiness is deep. Thrills are passing. Happiness is permanent. Happiness fills all our desires. But thrills are like a fix. The more we get, the more we want. Thrills are a narcotic, girls, that makes us greedy for more. Yet they never fill the emptiness in our souls."

His voice dropped to a confidential level. "Years ago, maybe we didn't dig this, huh? We played it cool. We spent our time trying hard not to be square. We lived on a cloud, tasting every pleasure. Now—isn't it true that deep down inside there's nothing we'd like better than a normal, square life?"

Deep sighs and solemn head nodding greeted this.

"And we can have that life," Father Egan declared, voice rising, "if only we remember that there's nothing we can't do by the strength of our wills if we want it strongly enough. But, if we want just those passing kicks instead of real happiness, then let's just waste our time hanging around this hospital rehashing all the dumb, stupid excuses for taking a fix the first day we get out of here.

"And we've heard all those excuses before, haven't we? But if we really want to do a little living and not just exist, if we really want to be square, then let's pray during the remainder of this Holy Mass for the courage, the wisdom and the grace to find a strong reason not to take that first fix."

He told them how, a few days before, he had been on the sixth floor of the House of Detention and had been spotted by one of his girls. She had given him a V-for-Victory sign and winked, and he had winked back at her. The sign and the wink had meant "Father, I'm free, I kicked it."

"And what she had also meant," he told his small audience, a hand chopping the air in emphasis, "was what Saint Augustine had said a long, long time ago. He said a good man is free, though he be a slave, and that a bad man is a slave, though he be a king. This girl was just explaining to me that even though she was behind bars, she was free. She was freer, probably, than the hack who was guarding her. Maybe the guard was drunk every night. Maybe she was a slave to alcoholism or something else. But the girl was saying that behind her bars she had made it, she had conquered junk, conquered lust, everything."

He nodded, slowing his words. "And girls, it's the same way with addiction. The only time we're going to be happy is when we can wake up in the morning and not reach for that needle. Then we'll be free, a slave to nothing and nobody. God bless you, girls."

He had begun to visit the hospital, a large, privately owned institution, when the city's Department of Hospitals initiated its treatment program for women addicts there. He had simply followed his girls to the hospital from the House of Detention, a short bus ride across town.

The hospital's solemn, brownstone exterior stretches the length of a block on Second Avenue. Its doors and street-level windows are as heavily barred as a medieval prison. An awning-covered entrance leads into a marble hallway where a plaque bearing the text of the Hippocratic Oath is mounted on one wall. A smaller entrance, on a side street, is painted black. It carries a white-lettered inscription:

SOCIAL SERVICE

This is the junkies' entrance.

Inside, in a colorless receiving room, addicts sit and nod and wait to be interviewed for admission. Often, in spite of the vigilance of hospital personnel, the city's ubiquitous narcotics pushers mingle with them. In swift, sleight-of-hand manner, small packages and crumpled bills change hands. Then, if they are so inclined, the addicts can use their furtively purchased drugs no more than a few feet away, in toilets adjoining the waiting room. To many addicts sex has long lost any meaning, and men and women inject heroin into their veins indiscriminately in each other's rest rooms.

Thus, when a patient is released from the hospital's two- or three-week detoxification program, he can resume the drug habit with little trouble. For only a few dollars heroin is available again before leaving the building. Once eleven girls were discharged from the hospital together after three weeks of careful and regular treatment. As they prepared to pass through the throng of addicts in the reception room, a voice whispered to them, "You wanna cop?"

"No," answered one girl. "No." She shook her head nervously, pleadingly.

"Come on." The voice was insistent. "I'll give it to you for three dollars."

The girls looked at each other. They hesitated and were lost. Quickly they pooled their pitifully few dollars and purchased enough heroin to begin the day.

Concerning the hospital, the 1962 report of the New York City Department of Hospitals said:

The program at this proprietary hospital was established on January 23, 1961, in response to a growing need, with an initial complement of 97 beds for male addicts. The treatment program provided by the hospital is under close supervision by the Department of Hospitals, financed through the Charitable Institutions Budget of New York City. Hospitalization is limited to the approximate two to three weeks necessary for complete withdrawal of drugs, or detoxification.

In 1962, 118 additional beds were placed in operation —on February 6, 43 beds were opened for women; on October 8, 50 beds were added for men to the 97 already in use and June 11, a fully approved unit of 25 beds for long-term treatment of adolescent female addicts was begun as a replacement for a similar program closed down at Riverside. The narcotics addiction treatment program in this proprietary hospital now consists of 215 beds—an increase of 82 per cent since it started.

The average length of stay in the hospital for an adult male, the report added, was 20.7 days. For an adult female it was 16.5 days. For an adolescent female, 50.7 days.

"Let me tell you what it's like to kick the habit in there, Father. They wake you at 6:30, and you get a dose of methadone in a bottle. It's pink. It tastes like soapsuds. Then you have another at ten o'clock and if you're in any kind of pain, which I was, they give you something for that too. Yeah, a painkiller."

The girl talked quietly and rapidly in the clamor of the Sixth Avenue luncheonette. The summer's night air outside was steaming. The city had been in the clasp of a heat wave for days. The sun had pressed down like a branding iron and at night the rock and stone of the streets seemed to exude the damp heat absorbed during the day. Inside the jammed restaurant the frigid air-conditioning was an almost exquisite relief.

"Then, Father," the girl continued, "you get another dose of methadone at 11:30. According to your habit, you get more or less. If your nerves are upset, you get a tranquilizer, too. At 4:30 another dose of methadone, then something else at six, then more methadone at nine. At ten o'clock you get your sleeping pills. But most of the girls don't sleep. They're up and around all night. Sometimes they play records but most of the time they talk junk.

"What else do they talk about? Nothing!

"Whose stuff are ya using? Where do you cop? How much are you usin'? Everybody using a thousand dollars' worth a day, natch. An' everybody in there's making a thousand dollars a day, natch. Except me. Times are hard, Father. When the workin' man ain't gettin' it, the hustler ain't gettin' it. 'Cause the hustler gets hers from the workin' man. But that ain't neither here nor there.

"Most of the girls in there got pretty morbid thoughts about men, anyway. Most of their troubles come from men. Well, anyway, the food is kinda monotonous. Chicken, ham, hard-boiled eggs, rolls, cereal, coffee. It's a good thing if you don't get real hungry in there, Father. But the doctors and people who work there ain't too bad. There's one doc who's reached the point, though, where he's just about given up. He thinks everybody is lyin' to him all the time. An' I guess some of 'em are. He's been working with addicts for a long time. He knows everybody. If I level with him, though, he helps me as much as he can. The only thing is, I wish I could get that kind of treatment without nothin' but junkies around me all the time. I don't want other people to know I'm an addict, but also I don't want to hear all that talk all day and night about drugs, drugs, drugs. It's no good for your morale. I go in there to try to kick a habit, not talk about one all the time. And the place is so confining, Father. It's depressing. To me it was miserable. Sometimes the girls fight with each other. One time they all broke into a medicine cabinet to try to get some stuff for themselves but the nurses came back in time. An' a girl was caught goin' through a nurse's pocketbook. So they put her out.

"An' all they talk about is how they can't wait to hustle again when they get out, an' all the junk they're gonna use. All they're waitin' for is the next shot to get high. I tell you, Father, when I got out of there I felt worse than I was when I went in. So I got a fix ten minutes later."

Father Egan nodded slowly, his lean face expressionless. He picked up the check for the two ice-cream sodas. They walked out into the stifling night.

As far as he was concerned, the girl had painted a vivid picture of how drugs dominated the consciousness of all in the hospital's addict wards. It was a picture identical to those drawn for him by many others.

The wards were a little Lexington, where patients talked endlessly of drugs, thought of drugs, probably dreamed of drugs.

Realization of this had been a major motivation for his continued visits to the hospital, in addition to hearing confessions and offering Masses. He felt the wards' inmates were assaulted by a constant barrage of "junkie talk," and he resolved to try to counter it.

For, during the 1950's, neither Lexington nor the city's Riverside Hospital, where addicted adolescents were confined together, appeared to be achieving even a minimally satisfying degree of success.

Father Egan and many others were convinced that at least one reason for this failure was the fact that addicts were being hospitalized at these institutions only with other addicts. They were therefore being subjected to a "cure" treatment in an environment only slightly removed from that which had been the cause of their addiction.

Narcotics hospitals as such, he concluded, were useless. Why should addicts not be placed in general wards, with patients suffering from other varieties of illnesses?

2

Riverside Hospital, on North Brother's Island in New York's East River, had begun in 1952 as a determined social and medical experiment with high hopes for its future. Legislation had been enacted by the State of New York enabling magistrates to commit adolescents aged sixteen to twenty-one to the hospital for up to three years. The hospital was well equipped and the city's Department of Education established a public school on its premises to aid in the rehabilitation process.

Efforts to stem the flow of smuggled narcotics to the hospital were not a total success. Some drugs were floated to the island in sealed containers, utilizing the surrounding water's swift currents. There were reports of parents bringing drugs to their children on visiting days.

Once a husky teen-age girl, desperate for drugs, plunged into the dangerously swirling currents separating the island from the Bronx mainland and swam, with miraculous success, to the shore. A vicious undertow ripped away her clothing and she crawled, naked and shivering, to a truck parked on the waterfront, within earshot of dock workers. She stole work clothing from the truck, including rubber boots ridiculously and pathetically too large, and somehow hobbled to a nearby apartment house and the relief of heroin.

In 1958 a team of researchers embarked on an evaluation study of Riverside. The study was conducted for the New York State Health Department by the Columbia University School of Public Health and Administrative Medicine. It was headed by a level-eyed, uncompromisingly dedicated physician named Ray Elbert Trussell, later a New York City Commissioner of Hospitals.

The research concentrated on the 247 patients admitted to Riverside for the first time during 1955. Data obtained was fascinating, occasionally shocking. It provided a penetrating inside view of the nature of the narcotics problem itself. Nothing like it, in scope and imagination, had been attempted before.

Of the 247 patients studied, 11 were dead. "A very high death rate for the age group in question," noted Dr. Trussell. Of the remaining 236, 147 were interviewed. Of these, *only 19 percent were found outside a prison or a hospital.* They talked, Dr. Trussell's report said, "freely and in the presence of a tape recorder."

Of the 247, 42 percent were listed as white, 26 percent Negro, 32 percent Puerto Rican. Eighty-three percent were male. Eighty percent were born in the Continental United States, 17 percent in Puerto Rico, 3 percent elsewhere. Seventy-one percent "stated an identity" with the Roman Catholic faith, 24 percent said they were Protestant, 5 percent said they were of the Jewish or other faiths. Eleven percent were married. Only 6 percent had finished high school—and 79 percent had not attended school for a year before entering the hospital.

"Psychiatric diagnoses were recorded for 96 percent of the group," the report added. "Forty-two percent were labeled as personality pattern disorder problems, 21 percent as psychotic."

The average age for beginning the use of marijuana or heroin was found to be 15.7 years.

When the researchers discovered what had happened to the youngsters after they were released from Riverside, their statistics jolted them afresh.

Of those without police records before admission to the hospital, 52 percent subsequently acquired such records.

Among those with one or two such prior offenses on their records, 65 percent were charged with new offenses after leaving the hospital. For those with three to seven entries on police blotters, the percentage soared to 83.

Fifty-one percent of all arrests were for narcotics possession; 24 percent were for theft.

Exactly 139 of the ex-Riverside patients, or 95 percent, admitted to returning to the use of narcotics following discharge; of these, 87 percent became readdicted.

The report's summary succinctly stated:

Any organized program dealing with the problem of drug addiction is faced with the historical fact that *no therapeutic success of any significance has ever been recorded.*

In the light of this reality the real question as to what should be done in organizing a program is one which can only be resolved on the basis of expert opinion insofar as immediate services to be provided are concerned, plus research, plus periodic appraisal of both service and research results.

Riverside Hospital, in other words, was a failure.

Eventually New York decided to close it. And a long-range policy decision was made to foster research into addiction— while at the same time trying to render a humane detoxification service to the addict in need of immediate relief.

The decision was translated into effective action by Dr. Trussell, who became the city's Commissioner of Hospitals in February, 1961. He came to his post from Columbia University where he had been Associate Dean for Public Health of the Faculty of Medicine. More than a year later he was to disturb many physicians in the New York area with a detailed report lashing their attitude toward some of the metropolitan region's medical problems. The report charged that "in the New York area, where the problems of the quality of medical care in New York State are among the worst, organized medicine is doing little about them."

Dr. Trussell, however, soon did a great deal about the narcotics problem.

"Regarding one aspect," he told the author, "I brought together the directors of medicine, the superintendents of my general hospitals, and asked them to admit a few female addicts to the open wards for detoxification. Nine of the hospitals agreed to do this. And one of them is so pleased at how well it has worked out that a paper was written on it."

But he added: "By and large most doctors and nurses do not like to work with an addict in an open ward, for a variety of reasons. There's the problem of drug security. There's the problem of pushers. There's the problem of the addict becoming increasingly restless as he goes off the drug. There are nurses who happen to have morphine around for people who are in pain and so on.

"On the other hand, if an addict is in a unit that's devoted to the problems of the addict he is handled by people who are used to working with addiction and who are committed to the field. If he's in an open ward where he's being treated along with fifty other patients with fifty other diseases, he's going to get the routine withdrawal treatment and a referral to a mental hygiene clinic and that's it.

"Of course, there are people who argue that the young addict going into a hospital filled with other addicts comes out knowing more places to buy the drug than when he went in. I don't know how cogent an argument that is for the simple reason that he knew where to get it in the first place or he wouldn't be in there. The fact is that some hospitals and aftercare centers and some community centers are used by some of these addicts to plan where they are going to get their next shot. And in fact some of them sneak into these places after nightfall and actually take the drugs.

"That doesn't mean we shouldn't go on trying to help them, but you have to be realistic about this problem. We've had relatively few complaints about our program of detoxi-fication on the open wards with the female addicts, although some of them have been troublesome. They pester the personnel. They want the next dose of methadone ahead of schedule. They try to manipulate the personnel. They'll wait until the nurse's back is turned or she's called away on emergency and they'll try to break into the drug box. That's one of the very real reasons why some people—not all—are reluctant to work with addicts.

"But I'm convinced the community has got to come to grips with this problem. The police are doing all they can. The medical profession has a very low rate of success when dealing with a really confirmed heroin addict. So research and prevention and humane detoxification are about all you're left with—plus some selective choosing of people who appear to be motivated to get well and with whom psychiatrists can work and help them get along in life with a minimum of drugs."

Perhaps one trouble was, as a leading New York physician

conceded, that actual physiological causes of addiction were not yet fully known. They were unknown, that is, to the extent where no pharmaceutical, chemical or even surgical cure had been devised to halt addiction as such.

In addition, the medical profession's success in motivating young persons to voluntarily abstain from narcotics had been little or none. Degrees of success appeared to be more marked as addicts became older, until the age of about fifty, when the ratio dropped again.

The author met one cheerful and resigned addict-prostitute aged fifty-seven. She said she had been refused detoxification treatment at a New York hospital by a doctor who told her she was "hopeless."

"And I guess I am, honey," she said, with a shrug. "But that's life, ain't it?"

3

Early in 1961 New York's program of "open ward" treatment of addicts finally got under way. And as one senior hospital department official put it, "It's difficult to deny that it was really a revolutionary change."

Many addicts who came for treatment had known little else but jail in the past; a cure meant writhing in cold turkey on a bare cell floor.

For others, with relatively minor habits, sudden withdrawal had not been so agonizing. They twitched, they scratched, they sweated, they became nervous and they had no appetite.

But regardless of the size of their habits, many who subsequently presented themselves for a "cure" said they were doing so because they felt for the first time that they were to receive medical attention on the same basis as any other sick person, with no police involvement.

The big question was, though: Would the program work? Was it indeed practical and wise to treat drug addicts in open wards both from the point of view of effectiveness of the treatment and from the effect on the hospital and other patients?

After a year's experience at least one New York hospital was sure it had the answer.

Coney Island Hospital is close to the famous boardwalk resort whose name it bears. It is occupied by about five hundred patients on an average day and is generally about 88 percent full. In 1962 more than eleven thousand persons were admitted as patients, suffering from the wide variety of illnesses found in most general hospitals.

When New York's "open ward" program for addicts began, Coney Island was among the first of the city's many hospitals to participate.

The senior medical superintendent of the hospital at the time was Dr. Eva Vandow. Together with Sally E. Knapp, M.S., Assistant in Administrative Medicine, School of Public Health and Administrative Medicine, Columbia University, Dr. Vandow wrote a remarkable account of the hospital's experience. It was entitled: "The Short Term Treatment of Narcotic Addicts in a Community Hospital." This was the paper referred to by Dr. Trussell in his comments on results of the city's moves into problems of hospital treatment of addicts. It was read with satisfaction and gratification by Father Egan, who saw in it a milestone on the path to a humane and effective approach to the entire drug problem—and a professional vindication of the layman's views he had been offering for so long.

What had happened at Coney Island Hospital, the paper explained, was this: A series of meetings designed to orient the hospital staff with the over-all narcotics question had been held. It was felt that if the idea of admitting addicts on a normal patient basis "could be sold as a worthwhile, exciting adventure to the medical staff, other objections could be easily overcome."

There were numerous reasons why hospital administrators had in the past, resolutely opposed such admittance of addicts. Most common of these were contentions that "special facilities" were needed, that "elaborate safeguards and special supervision" would be necessary, that drugs would be sold by hospital employees, that hostility would arise in wards on the part of non-addicts to addicts—and that addiction was "not curable."

At Coney Island it was, anyway, physically impossible to segregate addicts from other patients. There was neither the room nor sufficient nursing personnel to make this feasible. Dr. Vandow considered this "just as well" since it was felt that "addicts voluntarily seeking medical assistance would respond to being treated like patients instead of 'criminals.'"

Imbued with enthusiasm for the task, Coney Island took "desegregation" of addicts a stage further. They were transferred, once past acute stages of withdrawal and detoxification, to the hospital's rehabilitation service and were "encouraged to participate in all activities with rehabilitation patients, to work at occupational therapy projects, participate in recreation programs, be interviewed by the vocational guidance counselor, and attend group therapy sessions in the Medical Hygiene Clinic."

Other patients, it was observed, were "friendly and encouraging." Addicts responded "by helping to feed and transport handicapped patients."

The authors wrote:

Perhaps the greatest single criterion of the quantitatively small but qualitatively satisfying success of this hospital's program at the end of the first year is found in the appreciation expressed to the administrator by discharged addict patients and their families and by interested community agencies. If the administrator of any hospital, voluntary or governmental, will accept a few simple philosophies and face a few realities in the treatment of his addicts, his institution can render a real service. He must accept the fact that there is ample evidence to refute the popular belief that addicts are criminals *per se*, but rather that they are addicts first, who turn to robbery, murder and prostitution as a means of supporting their habit.

Nor should the financial consideration for admitting narcotic addiction patients be different from the criteria applied to other patients. They should pay for hospitalization when able to do so, but if medically indigent, should be given free care as members of the community. As a matter of fact, the cost per day for hospitalization of an addict may be less than average because of the fewer procedures required.

The administrator must realize that saying addiction is "not curable" forms no logical basis for refusal to admit these patients. Patients with other diseases also considered "incurable" are admitted and, in any case, complete abstinence on the part of the addict is not the only goal —there are degrees of addiction. A permanent "cure" should not be the criteria for successful patient care. At least two categories of addicts want to be helped: those who sincerely wish to "kick the habit" and those who wish to reduce their need to a point where it is a personal financial possibility without resorting to less savory means of obtaining money for the purchase of the drug.

The hospital administrator who gives way to feelings of frustration or sense of futility because his efforts can help, only to a limited extent, a limited number of human beings, is in the wrong "business."

After reading the paper Father Egan decided a major turning point in the battle had been reached. It remained to be seen how many other hospitals and administrators would see the problem in the same light.

When he accepted an invitation to speak to student nurses at Bellevue Hospital, also then admitting addicts to general wards, he decided to plead with them to look at addiction in the same way.

"Women have a certain Godly sensitivity," he told them. "Traditionally women make the most sympathetic nurses, the most understanding nurses. They have an ability to feel for their patients, to suffer with them.

"This, perhaps, is what addicts need more than anything —that certain sympathy. Don't, I beg you, give them that look of rejection, the look of disgust or suspicion that makes them feel that once a junkie, always a junkie, that no one trusts them, that everyone is suspicious of them.

"Please don't ever become so professional that you cease to be womanly. All an addict could need at a certain moment is one little word of encouragement. Nothing in the book says you can't tell an addict 'Oh, I see you're chucking today.' That's a junkie word. It means eating well. And believe me, girls, there's nothing more wonderful in the world than to see an addict, who maybe hasn't been interested in food for months, begin eating again."

Wryly, he suggested that perhaps they could occasionally "take a little initiative" and speak to the head nurse about patients who had no place to live when they left the hospital.

"You might be told that it's not the hospital's problem," he said. "But it must be *somebody's* problem.

"And to give you some encouragement," he concluded, "I can tell you I've had far more success in keeping addicts from returning to drugs if they've been held in the public wards here and in other hospitals than if they've made six or seven trips to Lexington. In an open ward addicts feel they're at least human beings. Otherwise they feel they're outcasts. But whatever they are they certainly need the kind of sympathy that often only nurses can give."

After his talk he had to hurry back to the Village. A girl had called him during the night, informing him that she was in serious trouble and that she had to see him immediately. He had dressed and met her in darkness at the corner of Sixth Avenue and Waverly Place. Her trouble had turned out to be acute heroin withdrawal symptoms and, clad only in blue jeans and thin shirt, she had trembled violently in the chill night air.

"Then let's try to get you into Bellevue," he urged. "It's warm in there, you can get a shot of methadone and you'll go to sleep and feel better in the morning."

She shook her head stubbornly. "Don't wanna go in no hospital."

"Then what do you want me to do?"

"Jus' loan me five bucks for a night's room rent, Father."

He sighed and handed her a five-dollar bill. She promised to repay him at 8 P.M. sharp, at the same place.

He drove rapidly to be on time for the appointment, concerned not for the money, but for the girl. The sidewalks were crowded but he spotted her waiting on the corner. He parked and walked toward her. One glance told him she was in no better condition than during the morning. The girl shrugged as if confirming his assessment.

"Ain't doin' so good, Father," she said. "I had to take a

fix twice today and I got to have more. I know when I can't fight it. And I sure don't have no money. But I got to get some an' there's only one way I can do that."

He shook his head. The evening Village crowds milled around them, some persons glancing curiously at the priest in deep conversation with the blue-jeaned girl.

"No, Lillian," he said. "No. Listen, if I get you something to take tonight will you promise me you'll go to Bellevue in the morning? At least to give it a try?"

The girl hesitated. She shrugged and nodded. "Yeah, if you can get it tonight, Father."

"But you promise me you'll come with me to Bellevue?"

"I promise."

He motioned to the girl to accompany him into Waverly Place, darker than brightly lit Sixth Avenue. In the shadows he handed her a small package. "Here," he said. "Methadone."

The girl slipped the package into a pocket. "I'll see you here at seven in the morning, Father," she said. "I promise I won't blow this chance. Trust me." She turned and disappeared in the crowds.

Watching her go, Father Egan was glad he had given her the pills, technically available only by prescription. It was better than knowing she was going back to prostitution and perhaps to jail. And besides, in an emergency it was clearly his duty to obey a higher law than the mere man-made kind.

For the lives they led placed them beyond the narrow confines of normality. Each girl had her story, as monstrous as it was unique.

10. THE GIRLS

FATHER EGAN had studied for the priesthood for ten demanding years. He had pored over principles applicable to every conceivable situation in life that could involve commission of sin. Murder, drunkenness, theft and rape were but a few. By the time he was ordained he felt nothing, *nothing*, could shock him.

Then he met his junkies.

He was not shocked. He was angered. No one, especially girls hardly more than children, should have been able to talk of such things.

For this is what they said. . . .

Name: Vicky Rinaldi
Occupation: None
Address: None
Age: 19

Father, it was in the slums of Brooklyn, in the neighborhood where I was born. Not many people were drug addicts there, but the ones I grew up with were all addicts. I was fourteen when I took my first shot.

I met some friends and they asked me if I wanted some fun. I said I did, because I was always game for kicks. So we went to a girl's apartment and there I got my first shot. I was deadly sick and I didn't like it.

But I had to find out what all this was about drugs, so I went back for more. My mother found I was associating with drug addicts so she took me to girl's court and they put me away.

Oh, I forgot. When I went away I was pregnant. I had my

baby at the reform school and they gave her to my parents. When I got out I was seventeen. I wanted my baby, but my parents acted like she belonged to them, not to me. So I packed up and walked out. Then a girl friend took me to a hotel in Manhattan. She dressed me up good first, and we met these guys. They were in their thirties and forties, well-spoken, and had a lot of money.

I got all excited when I saw all this money flashing around so I tried to make a play for one of the guys. And the guy liked me. He wanted to dress me up. Put me in his apartment. Give me anything. So I played along with him and he bought me a watch, rings, bracelets. Then he brought me lots of drugs and I started using it very heavily. I had a hundred-dollar-a-day habit. I was using cocaine and heroin and I felt I was in another world. I didn't want to know about anything, Father. He bought me beautiful clothes, this guy, and I never had less than two hundred dollars in my purse. I had everything a girl could want.

Then I started transporting the stuff. This guy was a racketeer, you see.

In the apartment he and his friends showed me a movie of airline pilots walking on a street. There were close-ups and everything, so I would get to know just what they looked like. They were bringing in the stuff. Then I had to go to the airport, using a name like Torchy or Lisa, or something like that. I had to wear a pink flower on a blue suit. Sometimes I had to wear a certain kind of glasses. One time I had to put on blue contact lenses. And when I'd meet him I'd have to take one off, so I would have one brown eye and one blue eye. Then he would know it was the right girl for sure. Another time they bleached my hair blonde, and on the front I had a dark strip. That was more identification. Also I had to wear a red scarf or a blue scarf around my neck. Or a pair of blue shoes. Or one glove. Or a fifty-dollar bill torn in half, and he would have the other half.

And I would go to the airport and bump into this guy like it was an accident. A couple of times I ran like I was trying to catch up with someone. When we bumped I would drop my suitcase and he would pick it up and hand me a package with it. Then I would head for the ladies' room, in case I was being followed. Inside, I used to change all my clothes. I had some other clothes in a key locker, just slacks and shirt or a sloppy sweater, so I would look like a kid. Then I would put an address and stamps on the package and mail it to the hotel. Never carried it from the airport, in case I was picked up.

Once I knew I was being followed, but I took three different cabs and lost them. But when I got back to New York later that night, they picked me up on the street and questioned me for eight hours. But they couldn't get nothing on me, Father. They had to let me go.

Well, anyway, I was getting two hundred and fifty dollars each time I made a pickup like that. Oh, sometimes I wouldn't mail it to the hotel, instead the package would go to some town in Connecticut or New Jersey or Pennsylvania.

Once I had to make a pickup in Key West, Florida. I flew down there, expenses paid and everything. I had a room all ready in a boardinghouse. I was told if the phone rang once and then stopped to leave and head back to New York. That meant something was wrong. If it rang three times, things were okay. It rang three times. So I brought six pure ounces of heroin back to New York, which is a lot of stuff, Father.

The toughest time I had was when I was sent on a job to Mexico City. I'm in the plane and I see this guy sitting near me. He was coughing like a sick junkie and nodding and all that. But he was dressed too good. He had new shoes on. Now all the guys with money in this racket don't use drugs. So this guy had dough—he had on a new mohair suit, too—and he was nodding and coughing. So it didn't add up. So he was a cop. It was easy.

When the plane got to Mexico City I lost him. I went to a rooming house in the slums. The mother had six kids and the husband was a bum. There was no food. By letting me stay there she got $500. She told me my connection was a man in a white suit, white hat and long cigar. But he never showed, because the feds came in an hour after I got there. I guess I didn't lose that guy at the airport after all. They searched the place and wrecked it. They took me to a station and a woman cop searched all my clothes. But they found nothing because I had nothing. Then they put me on the plane back to New York, and an American fed sat next to me all the way.

He bought me cigarettes and said he'd give me a thousand bucks if I would tell him who my big connections were. I told him he was crazy, that I was in Mexico visiting my future mother-in-law and that I was going to marry her son who was in New York.

He asked me why a nice Italian girl like me would want to marry a Mexican.

I said, love is funny, ain't it?

So he learned nothin' from me, Father. An' here I am, and what am I gonna do? Those guys I run with are mean.

My best girl friend, Gina, was killed by an overdose because she ratted on them. And we were close, like sisters. She was beautiful, beautiful. Never needed makeup. She looked like Kim Novak walking with a Marilyn Monroe build. Nobody could beat her in looks.

She wanted out from being with these guys. She wanted to get married. Her boyfriend was a square. You know what a square is—he didn't know nothing. He wanted her to give their names to the cops and get them arrested because they were no good for the community, and he wouldn't marry her unless she ratted on them. So these guys heard about this and they told her that if she married him she would rat to the cops. She promised she wouldn't and begged them not to do anything. But she said she loved her boyfriend and she had to marry him.

So they said okay, how about one more shot, just for the road? I was up there in the apartment when it happened. She went into the bathroom and took her shot. And when she came out, she said she was feelin' bad and she sat down on the bed.

I got nervous and I left. Next day I heard her body was found thrown from a car in front of a restaurant in Brooklyn. Her face, her beautiful face, was destroyed. They cut it up until it was raw, until she was unrecognizable. They had to identify her through her fingerprints. And the autopsy just said she was an addict who died of an overdose, an' that was that, Father.

So, what am I gonna do?

Name: Cathy Brennan
Occupation: Typist
Address: Irregular
Age: 20

I'm from right here in Manhattan, Father, from Hell's Kitchen. There were things that led up to it. My father raped me when I was twelve. My mother wouldn't believe me. She yelled at me to shut up in front of my younger brothers and sisters. It went on and on for three years until she found out. One day when he came in the room I left the window open and I screamed and screamed. So the neighbors called my mother up on the phone, and I ran out with my clothes torn and wearing one shoe, and my mother caught him. But nobody did anything about it.

I didn't know anything about dope to begin with. I was seventeen, a senior in high school. But when I graduated, my girl friend Trudy—she hated her father also but I don't know why—introduced me to a guy. He was actin' kind of giddy to me, and I thought he was maybe nuts. But one night he met me as I was comin' out of the beauty parlor and he said he wanted to talk to me about something. So we sat in the car and he told me he was smokin' marijuana and that was why he acted funny, because he was high. Did I want to try it? I said okay. And it made me forget my troubles at home.

So then, Father, I met another guy and he asked me if I would try heroin. I snorted it, you know, sniffed a little. Next night he turned me on all the way, with the needle. And, man, I liked it better than marijuana. Because with heroin I always know what I'm doing, Father. With marijuana, sometimes I couldn't think straight. So I kept staying with the junkies rather than the hopheads. What I liked about them most is that they never thought about sex, and with my memories of my father I didn't want to think about it, either. To me, that was why junk was the top blessing. It was like somebody dropped a godsend on my head.

I got a job as a secretary and I found I could keep working and still shoot a little now and then without trouble. I was just skin popping at first, you know, just shooting underneath the skin. But soon I started mainlining. And that I loved altogether because I could feel it right away. With skin popping it takes time, you have to wait. But with mainlining, you get it right away; it goes right into the vein and the bloodstream.

I had no money problems, either. This guy who turned me on paid for everything. He was a big pusher, maybe a dealer. Once we went to Florida for the winter. There were four guys and me and Trudy, and we had two pounds of heroin. We put it on the kitchen table to last us for the whole winter. We were the only six allowed in the house.

When I came back to New York my father had me put away as a wayward minor. I was still only seventeen. And when I came back, a year later, I had to get the stuff myself. My guy was gone.

So, let me see. Oh, yeah, I got married. To a junkie. I married him because my father had custody of me until I was twenty-one. The only way I could get out of that was to marry a guy over twenty-one. So he would become my legal guardian.

I started dealing in heroin. I'd go up to Harlem, up there between Lexington and Park to a tenement where nobody but dope addicts lived. Everybody knows it; it's a big shooting gallery. They shoot in the bathroom and the kitchens and the hallways. The cops are up there four and five times a day draggin' the people in and out.

One day I was in there and the cops come bustin' in the room and I ran down the fire escape. But a cop grabbed me at the bottom. I shoved the package of dope I had into my mouth and tried to swallow it. But he slugged me on the back of my neck and it fell out but it fell in the gutter where it had been raining and it all dissolved. So he had nothing on me; he just ran me in for disorderly conduct. Which was quite a break, Father.

Anyway I kept going up to Harlem with stuff and I never got caught. Then I decided to leave my husband. He beat me and hocked my television and he wouldn't do nothin' but lie around the apartment and shoot dope. I was doin' all the work.

He held up a jewelry store and the cops charged into our room at four o'clock in the morning. All I heard were a lot of sirens and a big crash and the next thing I knew there was flashlights in my face. At first I thought it was firemen and the building was burning down; but then I saw it was cops.

My husband says to the cops, will you please let my wife cover up? So they let me go in the bathroom and get dressed. The cops searched the place and found the watches my dumb husband had stolen; he put them under the mattress and that's the first place the cops looked.

So then I decided to quit him, which was a good thing. He's in jail someplace waitin' for his trial.

Next thing I meet an old boyfriend, Marty, from high school days. And he's on junk, too. But things looked up a bit—I got a job as a secretary in a research lab downtown. The place was loaded with morphine, so I kept Marty supplied with morphine. I was still dealing in junk, but only keeping enough for myself.

But Marty's parents were sick at heart over their son. They gave him some money and begged him to leave town, to go to Mexico, Chicago, anywhere, as long as he would keep away from his junkie friends. I was sorry he was leaving, because Marty was wonderful. Everybody loved him. No one ever said a mean word about him. Other guys got mean once in a while; Marty never got mean. No one ever beat him up; he never beat anyone up. He was always free with his money, even when he needed a fix real bad. If there was another junkie who was sick, Marty would share all he had with him. He was an unbelievable person. He was more or less a junkie saint.

So before he was to leave town, Marty and me and Trudy and two other guys were in this apartment up on Central Park West, in the Nineties.

Marty has his own syringe. A regular syringe like doctors have, with a disposable needle. Not the cheap eyedroppers and needle like we use, Father. He got it from his grandfather who was a diabetic. So, anyway, we're takin' our turn using the stuff and Marty got jumpy and said he couldn't wait. I know how he felt; you can die there sitting and waiting while the others are shooting.

He kept saying to me, how's the stuff, Cathy? I said, it's nice, Marty. Then he said he would have to use his own stuff;

he couldn't wait any longer. I told him to be careful. So he
went in a corner for a minute and came back and told me to
hold the belt around his arm.

I asked him how much he had in that needle. He told me
not to worry about it; he just wanted to be hit. He had a little
trouble finding the vein, and I even helped him with it.

Then he went and sat down in a chair.

Suddenly Trudy said to go slap Marty in the face; he
didn't look so good. He didn't; he looked like he was passin'
out. And Marty heard her and mumbled that he was all
right. But I saw he was in trouble.

I ran over to him and with one of the guys lifted him out
of the chair. His body went rigid; his fists clenched.

The guy hollered, *Walk him, walk him!*

But he did a backbend that knocked us both on the floor.
I let out a scream tellin' the others, *For Pete's sake, get the
hell over here!* But they were more concerned with stickin'
that needle in their arms.

I got a wet cloth and put it on Marty's face. He went purple and blue and black and orange. He was leaning up
against the wall in a sitting position and I loosened his belt
and his sleeves and his neck and took off his sweater.

Then the others came over and started slapping him and
pouring water over him. Everybody was working on him.
We started giving him artificial respiration; we didn't know
what to do.

All of a sudden he started to breathe fast, but it was a
funny breathing. Then it stopped. Then it started again.

His eyes were closed and when I opened them they were
in the back of his head.

Trudy and one of the guys got nervous and said they were
gettin' out of there. I screamed at them that Marty was sick,
that they couldn't leave him.

Yeah, but if he dies, we'll be up for murder, they hollered
back. So I told them to get out, and that I would stay. I said
he was real sick, that I'd seen people with overdoses before.
But they left, all except one of the guys, a colored guy, who
said he would stay.

He picked Marty up and put him on the bed. He was still

breathing off and on. Marty began to choke, so I grabbed his tongue because I didn't want him to swallow it.

I started yellin' that I'd never seen anyone this bad before. I was going out of my mind.

Then Marty started getting more purple and blue. And the colored guy turned him over gently, like he was a baby, and gave him more artificial respiration, while I held his head.

Suddenly his body shook all over and this stuff started comin' out of his nose. It was like a red foam, like bloody foam. Then he foamed at the mouth and everything seemed to relax and we knew he was dead.

Somehow I didn't panic. The colored guy picked him up in his arms and we took him upstairs to the fifth floor and put his body in the bathroom. Then we went down to the third floor and back in the apartment.

Soon we heard an ambulance and the cops came. Somebody had found poor Marty. But because he was dead the ambulance didn't take him. They put a cop there to wait for the coroner. It was eleven o'clock on Saturday night when he died and the coroner didn't come until nine o'clock Sunday night. Marty lay the whole time on the concrete bathroom floor. These things were so common in that neighborhood that nobody got excited over a dead junkie.

We cleaned up the apartment and got out of there the next day. I figured maybe Marty's death would hit me later, but it didn't. It never did. It was just part of the life I was leading and had to be expected. When I think of Marty today, I don't even think of him as dead. Maybe if I had gone to his wake it would be different.

So I felt pretty bad after that, Father. I lost my job. I even went to a priest in my parish and asked him for money. I told him I had to have it for my mother because my father was drinking up his paycheck. It wasn't for that, of course. It was for dope. But this priest knew me from my neighborhood; he was no square. He told me to come see you. I thought about it awhile and went to see a doctor instead.

He gave me pills to stop me from sweating, to keep my nose from running, to stop my diarrhea and my cramps. He gave me something to help me sleep at night. But nothing did me any good, and he wouldn't prescribe dolophine. I told him he had me taking all these things, this one every three hours, that one every four hours, this one eight times a day, the other one twice a day, another one in the middle of the night. And all of them put together were only making me sicker. I tried and tried to stay off drugs, but I couldn't hold out. I couldn't stand on my two feet.

I got another job typing in an office. It's the only thing holding me together. But I still have to deal in junk to keep myself going. Yet I have to keep the job, for if I quit it takes me a long time to get up and find another one. You know, I get all involved with shooting heroin all the time.

So finally I decided to take my priest up on his advice and come and see you. So here I am, Father.

Name: Toni McClain
Occupation: None
Address: None
Age: 22

I got nothin' to tell you, Father. When I was ten I ran away from home and that made my parents mad. Because it made the school authorities come and investigate our home, up in Yonkers. And they decided we were being neglected so they took me and my brother and sister and put us in a special home for kids. My father never came home and my mother had run off with a boyfriend, so I guess we were in pretty bad shape. We were more or less left alone most of the time.

So I ran away from the home and they caught me and put me in a boarding school where it was very strict but nice and clean. And I ran away from there and found my mother and the cops picked me up again. I was twelve at the time, and I wanted to be with my mother. But they sent me to a New York State reformatory, a training school for girls. Except you don't learn nothing much, you know how kids are. I first heard about marijuana there.

I ran away from there several times. I hitchhiked a ride into the city with a truck driver. I got in the truck and the driver gave me some money. That was the first time I was a prostitute. I was thirteen.

When I got to New York I didn't know anyone. I just rode up and down in a bus. And, you might have known it, as the bus was going through Harlem I saw this girl I had been with in the reformatory. So, seeing a familiar face, I jumped off and stayed with her awhile. She was living with her mother, you know.

But my friend was running with a pretty fast crowd. Older people. And I started snorting cocaine. I was at an after-hour place where they sold whiskey and marijuana and what have you, and this fellow came over and asked us if we wanted to get high.

Naturaly, I didn't want to be a square. I was young and I wanted to be up-to-date with everyone else. So I accepted. I snorted the cocaine. You sniff it through your nose, Father. It was a stimulating feeling. Cocaine was three dollars for a capsule, and the two of us could get high for a couple of hours on it. Then I discovered there was something else called H.

A guy said to me that H was only one dollar a capsule. So I bought it; it looked the same as cocaine. I didn't know what it was, I didn't even know H stood for heroin. I snorted it, and got quite nauseous. But I had to stick it out because nobody else got sick. So I had to make the best of it. Then I found it was habit forming. It didn't bother me at first. I figured biting your nails is a habit too, and so what? I just took it to be part of the crowd.

I got arrested when I was fourteen for prostitution, but they let me go. So things went on like that for a while. I was using heroin and picking up a few dollars wherever I could and living with my girl friend.

When I was seventeen they arrested me again. Yes, for prostitution. I was sent upstate to Westfield for three years, but got out after sixteen months on parole. I picked up this guy at Fifty-Fourth Street and Seventh Avenue and the cops followed me and arrested me. So I was sent back to Westfield to finish my time. And when I came out I was through with snorting heroin. I started mainlining it for real now.

I met a girl from Westfield and she showed me how. She even put the needle in for me until I learned how to do it myself. And I used heroin steady that way for more than a year. I never even had a chance to get sick, I used so much.

Then I got pregnant. The baby's father was a dope connection, a pusher. He supported my habit, gave me stuff for free while I was carrying the baby. He didn't want me to go out and hustle. My baby was born with the habit, born addicted.

They took me to Lincoln Hospital in the Bronx when my time was near. I didn't tell the doctors I was an addict, because I had it set up for drugs to be brought to me while I was in the hospital. And I knew that if they discovered I was an addict they would place a watch on me. But when the baby was born, they couldn't figure out what was wrong with her.

She couldn't sleep. She couldn't hold anything on her stomach. She was twitching, jumpy, perspiring and had diarrhea. Finally I had to tell them it was because I was an addict. Then they gave the baby paregoric, I guess, to let the baby down gradually from the habit. She was so cute and little, only weighing five pounds at birth.

When I left the hospital I went right back on drugs. The baby's paternal grandmother took my baby to raise her and I've never seen her since. I wish I could. But maybe it's just as well, considering the life I lead.

Like the other night when I was going into a hallway up in the Nineties near West End Avenue. I was going there to buy some drugs in an apartment upstairs. On my way up some fellows grabbed me and beat me with their fists, punching me all over, on my chest and everywhere. They kicked me and one guy took a belt with a metal buckle and slugged me with it. See—where I have the cut under my eye? I finally managed to get out of there. They didn't have much luck with me because I carried on too loud. I screamed and hollered and they got scared. Outside, in the street, I stopped a patrol car and told the cops what happened. They told me it was my fault and that I should stay away from that building.

So I went down to Ninety-Sixth Street to meet a girl friend and ask her to come to hospital with me so I could get my eye stitched. I found her and she ran into a cafeteria to get a paper napkin for my eye—the blood was running down my face—and a police car pulled up and the cops picked us up for disorderly conduct.

From the station house they sent me to hospital to get my eye looked at. Then I went to jail for three days. When I got out I was picked up again, also for disorderly conduct. Just regular pickups, you know. I know all the cops and they all know me. This time I got thirty days. When I got out I went back to Ninety-Sixth Street and got picked up again the same night. What for? Nothing. Just because they know me. And I went back to the House of D. and was out fifteen days later. A great life.

That night, about ten o'clock, I was having coffee in a restaurant uptown with some fellow. We were both pretty high on goofballs at the time, Father. Some other guys started getting fresh with me and I got nasty, too, because the goofballs make you think you're smart.

Well, the guy I was with told them to leave me alone. So one of the other fellows pulled a knife and stabbed him in the back. I ran out to get some help and those characters chased me along the sidewalk. It was warm weather and all the people were out, sitting on the benches and all.

When they caught up with me they threw me down on the sidewalk and began stabbing me. So I'm getting treated now for a punctured lung, a stab in my back, one under my left breast, the outside of my arm, the inside of my arm and my left leg. It happened in front of hundreds of people and when the cops came nobody said they saw anything.

But one guy, I don't know who he was, must have seen it all. He was the one who called you, Father. And it was the first time I met you.

Father Egan had received the call a few minutes before going to bed. A Spanish-accented male voice told him a girl named Toni McClain, an addict, had been knifed by some of his friends and that she had been taken to Bellevue.

At the emergency room he had asked for her by name, and a doctor had shrugged ominously. Toni was on the critical list. But she smiled feebly when he sat by her side and whispered that he shouldn't worry about her, she would make it okay.

Hours later, when she was stronger, he was still at her side. He explained he was Father Egan, probably well known to some of her friends. Toni nodded philosophically.

He returned to the hospital the following day and heard her confession.

Later Toni told him, "It's been a wasted life, really. Very disgusting. I haven't done anything with my life. Nothing to show for it."

In reply he gave her a packet of cigarettes and two dollars.

"I got sort of all choked up about this," Toni remembered saying. "I just felt like crying all the time. Nobody ever showed an interest in me before. Not even my earliest memories, when I was home with my mother."

When Toni was released from the hospital Father Egan found her a hotel room on downtown Broadway, as far away as possible from Ninety-Sixth Street.

A few days later she disappeared. When he found her again she was back in jail.

"I had to go uptown, Father." She shrugged. "I just had to. I belong up there. It's where I know everybody and where everybody knows me. It's home. Everybody looks bad up there and I don't have to feel ashamed of myself or self-conscious all the time. Everybody's in the same predicament as me; they're goofball artists, junkies, what have you. Well, a day or so later I picked up this guy on the street. He looked regular enough, you know, he asked me how much I wanted and I asked him how much he had. This went on back and forth for a while like it always does. You know, if you ask for a hundred you come down to twenty-five an' if you ask for twenty-five you come down to ten. The next thing I know he pulls a badge on me. He's a cop. So I go back to the Twenty-Fourth Precinct and it's like old home week. I say, hello fellers, what's new? Then I guess I passed out because I woke up in Bellevue with my stomach pumped out. Then I spent the night in jail and went to court and got another fifteen days and when I get out I guess I'll get busted again an' get another stretch and so on and so on. . . .

"*Say, Father, d'you think it'll ever end?*"

11. WOMEN'S COURT

1

PART NINE of the Criminal Court of the City of New York, better known as Women's Court, is conducted in a modern, high-ceilinged courtroom with light paneling covering its walls. A United States flag stands beside the judge's high-backed chair, adding color to the room's subdued tones. High above the chair, on paneling behind the bench, are inscribed the gold-lettered words IN GOD WE TRUST. The court is decorous and air-conditioned and in these respects is identical to other courtrooms in the vast, bustling Criminal Courts Building on Centre Street, a crowded artery of Lower Manhattan. Women's Court, however, contains an important difference. A tall screen stands behind the first row of spectator seats, blocking the view into the courtroom from its unlocked, windowed doors. The public is not encouraged to observe the court's proceedings.

Looking as if they had spent the night in jail, indeed as most had, the morning docket of women and girls entered the courtroom in drab procession as each name was called. They appeared from a polished door beside the bench; beyond the door was a prisoners' waiting room from where the sound of clanging iron doors could be heard. It was Saturday morning, when arraignments were held. The women faced their encounter with justice with varying degrees of comprehension, plus expressions of stony blankness, cynicism or apathy for the judge, the uniformed court officer and the throng of short-sleeved, sport-shirted police officers with silver shields pinned to their chests.

The first girl, in green slacks and sweater, hair uncombed, approached the bench. The court officer was intoning the charges.

". . . the defendant offered to commit an act of prostitution with the deponent for the sum of eight dollars."

The deponent, the police officer who had arrested her, stood phlegmatically at her side.

". . . you have the right to communicate with friends or relatives free of charge by letter or telephone and the right to counsel at this stage of the proceedings or further proceedings," the court officer continued. He spoke rapidly and mechanically, as a man does who has uttered the same words thousands of times.

The judge leaned forward. Carefully, he asked the defendant if she understood the charge.

"Yeah, I think so," she said doubtfully.

"Would you like a postponement?"

"Huh?"

"A postponement. Would you like your case put off to a later date? The court will provide you with a lawyer free of charge if you are unable to afford one yourself. Or do you wish to plead guilty?"

"I don't know."

"Well, what do you want to do?"

"I don't know."

The judge sighed. He advised the girl to accept a postponement, when free counsel would be available. She shrugged and nodded.

"Bail $500," said the judge. "Next case."

A pony-tailed blonde girl with chalk-white features entered the courtroom.

". . . she demanded and received a set of bongo drums and two stereo records," droned the court officer. "The officer proceeded to the apartment having paid the sum of $16.50 for the items. There she said she would not ask for cold cash, because she merely wanted some things for the apartment."

"All lies," snapped the girl. She glanced bitterly at the impassive detective at her side.

"Bail $500," said the judge. "Next case."

Father Egan attended Women's Court regularly; often a girl would need his help after being arrested during the night. And a judge would release her, care of Father Egan, and he would arrange for her to be sent to Lexington.

He detested Women's Court. To his legally unsophisticated mind it seemed outrageous that women were constantly found guilty on the word of arresting officers alone, without witnesses or other corroboration. Usually their protests were on the lines of: "Father, sure I was on the street. But I hadn't done anything when the officer arrested me. I know when I've been arrested fairly and this wasn't it. I hadn't approached anyone, even if it was only because there was no one to approach. Yet the same officer who arrested me last month arrested me again. But I can't plead innocent. I've got a police record. If I plead guilty I'll get thirty or sixty days. If I plead innocent and go to trial they may throw the book at me. I could get six months or a year. So I'll plead guilty, though I did nothing."

The demanding and accepting of funds or gifts frequently figured critically in these cases. He recalled one girl tearfully demanding of a judge, "If he gave me the money, as he said he did, where is it? Where is the money? They searched me at the station house and took everything away from me. So where's the money he said I accepted from him?"

She was jailed. And another aspect of the law arose to puzzle and anger him. They went to jail, their clients went free. But why shouldn't every man who patronized them be equally considered as a lawbreaker? He was clearly implicated in the offense. Women did not force men to accompany them. Why should an eighteen-year-old girl be sentenced to one to three years in prison while her client went free?

Troops of addicts filed through the criminal courts each day, charged with sale or possession of drugs, theft and prostitution. In a single year seven thousand persons were arrested in New York for possession, virtually all of them addicts.

Father Egan sat in court and watched the same faces reappear. It was a frustration shared by an individual of no less legal stature than Judge John J. Murtagh, Administrative Judge of the Criminal Court of the City of New York. For Judge Murtagh had written:

. . . experience plainly shows that the attempt to legislate addiction out of existence is generally futile. Besides, the enforcement program has done much to sustain organized crime and creates occasions for the corruption of enforcement officers. Our present policy, therefore, is of questionable value.

Perhaps nowhere is the cruelty of the police more evident than in the Criminal Court of New York City. As many as fourscore addicts confront a judge on a single day. In his heart, the judge knows there is little or no hope for any of them. Yet he must go through the motions of supporting an enforcement program which, he is convinced, is creating more serious problems than it solves.

Addiction is a condition of human degradation. It cries out for humane tolerance and Christlike charity. But these, unfortunately, are not the qualities that we now bring to the problem of addiction. The time has come to reassess our approach to the problem.

2

At least one consequence of this "present policy" was apparent inside the House of Detention. Like many jails, the House was, in effect, two prisons. One held those who were serving sentences after conviction in court. The other held those awaiting trials due to their inability to raise bail.

"This would not happen to the average person, with a job and a normal life," Father Egan would observe. "If such a person were arrested, for whatever reason, mistakenly or legitimately, he or she would call someone and be immediately bailed out. But if you've got no family, or if your family's got no money, you stay there."

They stayed in the House of Detention for periods ranging from several weeks to a year and more.

"Take a typical case," Father Egan said. "A girl had her bond set at five hundred dollars, a frequent figure in Women's Court. She needed twenty-five dollars to get the five hundred from a bondsman. She called her mother. Her mother was living on welfare payments; she had four small

children to worry about besides this headache of a daughter.
And the Welfare Department doesn't make allotments for
bail money. But somehow mama got up the twenty-five and
took it to a bondsman. He said that was fine, it would pay for
the bond. But what about collateral? Mama shrugged and
walked away. Yet the bondsman, a product of the system
himself, couldn't be blamed. He stood to lose his five hundred."

Inequities of the bail system had not gone unnoticed. In
1961, in fact, a special study was begun to examine the possibility of an alternative system. Students from the New York
University School of Law and staffers of the Vera Foundation questioned large numbers of defendants to learn more
about the plight of the indigent accused. Concerning this
study, the National Council on Crime and Delinquency published a booklet, by Charles Ares, associate professor of
law at N.Y.U., and Herbert Sturz, executive director of the
Vera Foundation. It said of the bail system:

> The bail decision is usually made at the defendant's
> first appearance before a magistrate. A prosecutor is
> there and he may be accompanied by the arresting offi-
> cer. No one speaks for the indigent accused unless he
> happens to be lucky enough to be arrested in the few
> jurisdictions where legal aid or a public defender system
> provides representation at this point. Even there assigned
> counsel, for lack of time, can do little for the defendant
> so far as bail is concerned. The magistrate usually relies
> on facts presented by the prosecution and police, whose
> interests in the amount of bail may not coincide with the
> defendant's.
>
> Assuming the bail has been set in a reasonable
> amount, who ultimately decides whether the defendant
> obtains his release? Curiously, at this point in the crim-
> inal process the decision-making power is lifted from a
> public official and deposited in the hands of a private
> person whose discretion is unfettered and whose decision
> is final—the bail bondsman. He may deny freedom to
> the accused for lack of the premium or collateral, or
> for whim.

A study of bail administration in New York City conducted in 1958 showed that, in the cases studied, 28 per cent of those defendants whose bail was set at $500 could not make it; 45 percent were unable to raise bail when it was set at $2,000.

And former Attorney General Robert Kennedy said, in 1961: "I have a strong feeling that the law, especially in criminal cases, favors the rich man over the poor in such matters as bail, cost of defense counsel, the cost of appeals and so on."

Father Egan tried, with occasional success, to circumvent the bail system by asking judges to release women and girls on their own recognizance, adding that he would vouch for their appearance in court. An increasing number of judges became inclined to do this.

3

At one preliminary hearing he was convinced the accusing officer could have mitigated the charge against a woman defendant in a narcotic case. After she had pleaded guilty he approached the officer.

"That girl swore on her own children's lives that she didn't do everything you said," he whispered. "She didn't deny the charge, just some of the circumstances. You could have made it easier for her."

The officer stared at him implacably. "It was her word against mine," he said. "And anyway, Father, don't take the problems of society on your shoulders."

Father Egan knew the officer was right. His word weighed more heavily than hers. He was a police officer entrusted by the city with a badge and a gun to enforce its laws. He had no criminal record. He was not illiterate. He was not disheveled after a night in jail. He did not shuffle into the courtroom suffering from heroin withdrawal. He was not in too much physical or emotional distress to be able to, or even want to, pay attention to the court's proceedings.

Father Egan finds it difficult to blame many of his girls

for bitterness toward police. But he demurs at their frequent assertion that there is "no such thing as a good cop."

"My father is a retired police officer," he points out mildly. "He was a good cop all his life."

Officers with whom his girls frequently come in contact are members of the Narcotics Bureau of the New York City Police Department. The bureau is housed in a dingy set of offices in a Lower Manhattan precinct building. It was the building that Father Egan had visited when he first became interested in the narcotics problem. The bureau is made up of one hundred and sixty carefully chosen officers. The bureau remains untainted by scandal, a fact attributed by a former commander to the caliber of its personnel, in daily contact with quantities of drugs often worth large fortunes. One senior officer, in fact, considers them the finest men and women on New York's huge force. They operate frequently undercover, in disguises ranging from hot dog salesmen to Santa Claus, and often in garb rendering them indistinguishable from inhabitants of the city's most drug-ridden neighborhoods. They are feared by New York's addicts, pushers and narcotics racketeers.

This does not prevent Father Egan from occasionally recognizing a disguised policeman on the street and amusing himself by greeting him with a loud, "Hi, officer!" to the man's agitated annoyance.

Narcotics officers pride themselves on their knowledge of the narcotics problem and the means of coping with it. Their views are, with few exceptions, in sharp contrast to those held by such individuals as Father Egan.

While social causes of addiction are under examination, while counseling, gradual detoxification, psychiatry and various forms of therapy are in increasing use in the addiction field, most narcotics officers are convinced that the "police approach" to the problem, the approach of stern law enforcement, is the best and most effective one.

"This is cops' business," a veteran officer insisted. "We're in this thing up to our necks every day. We deal with the most conniving, vicious element in the city. We understand them."

He opened the drawer of a steel cabinet in his office. It

was crammed with files on Father Egan, the New York Council on Narcotic Addiction plus other individuals and civic groups concerned with the problem. He flipped a finger through the files, then abruptly closed the drawer.

"No," he said, "we honestly don't believe those kind of efforts do any good. The cops do it better."

He tossed a neatly typed report on his desk.

"Addicts sick people?" he asked derisively. "They should be treated with sympathy and kindness? Take a look at this!"

The report described how a number of narcotics officers had been injured while effecting recent arrests.

1. On March 7, 1963, a detective was punched in the face and knocked to the ground by a prisoner. It was necessary for the officer to draw his revolver and fire a warning shot to subdue his prisoner. The detective sustained a broken nose.
2. On February 28, 1963, a detective was conducting a narcotics investigation of a subject in an auto. The suspect attempted to run the officer down with the auto and drove away. The detective followed, overtook him, and after placing the man under arrest was assaulted by the prisoner.
3. On February 14, 1963, a detective was entering an apartment on a narcotics investigation when he was attacked and bitten by a dog owned by the suspect.

Other incidents told of narcotics detectives being kicked, punched, attacked with knives, knocked down flights of stairs and threatened at gun point. Most police officers would agree, however, that such experiences were not confined to narcotics detectives. A New York City police narcotics report, dated April 8, 1963, noted: "In general, users made up a higher proportion of persons arrested for crimes associated with property in both 1962 and 1961 than they did of persons arrested for crimes against the person."

It is true that in 1962, 7.6 percent of persons arrested for murder were found to be users, as compared to 4.2 percent in 1961. Yet this also meant that 92.4 percent of those arrested for murder in 1962 were *not* users.

The report was based on a study of the 207,615 persons arrested by New York City police for all types of crime in 1962. Of these, 13,670 (12,633 males; 1,037 females) "used narcotics or other types of drugs." The study noted that 6.6 percent of all persons arrested in the city in 1962 were narcotics or drug users. The percentage was 5.9 in 1961.

The report also disclosed percentages of drug users among the various categories of arrests: Rape, 1.2; robbery, 9.2; felonious assault, 1.7; burglary, 16.2; grand larceny (other than motor vehicles), 14.9; grand larceny of motor vehicles, 3.4; sale or possession of narcotics as a felony, 75.3; possession of narcotic drugs or implements as a misdemeanor, 85.3.

The percentages aroused considerable interest. They appeared to refute the widely held belief that the addict population was mostly responsible for the city's many brutal crimes "against the person." The extremely low percentages of addicts among those seized for rape and assault (1.2 and 1.7) —with an estimated 30,000 or more addicts in town—did, in fact, tend to support wearily repeated contentions of Father Egan and others that the drug addict was the least violence-prone of lawbreakers.

The Narcotics Bureau, moreover, had its recommendations for dealing with the drug problem:

1. Legislation which will provide certainty and severity of punishment, after conviction, for non-addict sellers of narcotics.
2. Compulsory registration of addicts.
3. Adequate hospitalization and treatment for addicts which would include an adequate aftercare and rehabilitation program.
4. Education of the populace through the schools, churches, social agencies, etc., on the evils of addiction, with emphasis on depicting the horrible aspects of it.
5. More stringent enforcement against the smuggling of narcotics from foreign lands.
6. The enactment of protocol within the United Nations by [drug] growing nations which will control the growth of opium and the manufacture of illicit drugs.

7. Cooperation by the federal government and the states in effecting a program of coordination and cooperation in combating this evil.

Some senior narcotics officers, nevertheless, were privately skeptical of the feasibility of rehabilitation and of the value of educating "the populace." In addition, they felt that while compulsory registration of addicts was desirable, compulsion should be taken even further. Addicts, they said, should be committed to "health camps" in rural areas, far from the city's influence. There "they should be placed under Army-style discipline—it would be the finest thing in the world for them; it would straighten their backs and give them self-respect and dignity."

Father Egan had his reservations about the "health camp" suggestion and the compulsory registration provision of the bureau's program. He felt the addict had experienced enough incarceration and compulsion, with few results except bitterness and failure.

In apparent paradox, he is regarded in high esteem by the Federal Bureau of Narcotics, a body famed—and blamed—for relentless enforcement of federal narcotics laws. From his earliest days of preoccupation with the drug problem, since his meeting with Commissioner Anslinger, Father Egan and the federal bureau have enjoyed a close and amicable relationship. First through Anslinger, then through his successor, Commissioner Henry Giordano, Father Egan has managed, in emergencies, to bypass normal channels and gain swift admittance for addicts to the federal hospital at Lexington. The relationship flourishes even though Father Egan has opposed some of the federal bureau's policies as vehemently as he has done those of the New York City police. Anslinger noted this when he wrote the author from retirement at Hollidaysburg, Pennsylvania. He stated he had "profound admiration" for Father Egan, and described him as a "courageous fellow." Anslinger added that "although he does not agree entirely with my views, I have the highest regard for him." He said that Father Egan was the "only" priest "who gave us any assistance."

At the bureau's New York office, in the federal building

at 90 Church Street, George H. Gaffney, assistant to the commissioner, and Samuel Levine, the bureau's district superintendent at Philadelphia and a longtime acquaintance of Father Egan, voiced the same opinion: "There aren't enough like him."

Yet the federal bureau has every characteristic of a tough police agency. (Nevertheless, all addicts interviewed by the author were emphatic in stating that if they had to be arrested, they always hoped it was by federal, not local, officers.)

In the lobby of its New York office stands a tall display cabinet, its top shelves crowded with awards for pistol shooting, won by the bureau in inter-police organization contests. On lower shelves are knives, pistols, scissors, clubs and longshoremen's hooks, presumably seized in narcotics arrests. In a corner of the cabinet stands a green bottle and a thin colored cylinder. A white card beside it reads: HASHEESH PIPE *(Used in Morocco)*. In another corner lies a glass eyedropper with a hypodermic needle attached. Two other needles lie beside it. A card next to them reads:

THIS NEEDLE AND SYRINGE SEIZED FROM [here it named a well-known television personality] AT THE TIME OF HIS ARREST, WHEN HE WAS FOUND HIDING IN A HALLWAY TOILET. HE IS AUTHOR OF [named were two books written by the performer].

For years the Federal Bureau of Narcotics had been the subject of controversy between those who insisted on stringent antinarcotics laws and those who favored a tolerant approach to the plight of the addict. Operating under the Treasury Department, the bureau, however, merely insisted it was meeting its responsibilities of enforcing federal legislation with respect to narcotic drugs.

Before 1914 no such legislation existed. Then Congress passed the Harrison Act, a regulatory statute aimed at controlling the distribution of drugs. In succeeding years the Treasury Department came under increasing criticism for seeming to enforce the statute as if it were prohibitory, not regulatory. In a case involving the conviction of a physician for alleged illicit dispensation of drugs to an addict, however, the United States Supreme Court noted the Harrison Act "says nothing of addicts and does not undertake to prescribe methods for their medical treatment. They are diseased and proper subjects for medical treatment and we cannot possibly conclude that a physician acted improperly or unwisely or for other than medical purpose solely because he has dispensed one of them, in the ordinary course and in good faith, four small tablets of morphine or cocaine for the relief of conditions incident to addiction."

The physician's conviction was reversed. But subsequently many members of the medical profession appeared to be terrorized into adopting a "hands off" policy to the treatment of addiction. The prohibitory concept of antinarcotics legislation seemed to become the accepted one. Arrests and convictions of addicts spiraled and new and tougher laws appeared on statute books.

On July 25, 1962, the Supreme Court reversed this trend in abrupt and historic fashion. Striking down a California statute making it an offense to be a drug addict, the court ruled, in effect, that addiction was a sickness and not a crime. By a vote of six to two the court declared the statute violated the "cruel and unusual punishment" provisions of the Constitution. Justice Potter Stewart wrote the majority opinion and was joined by Chief Justice Earl Warren and Justices Hugo L. Black, William O. Douglas and William J. Brennan. Justice John Marshall Harlan invalidated the statute as "arbitrary" but not as cruel and unusual punishment. Dissenting opinions were written by Justices Tom C. Clark and Byron R. White.

The case had involved a Los Angeles arrest. Police stopped a man one night and discovered needle marks on his arm. He was sentenced to ninety days in jail.

"To be sure," Justice Stewart's opinion stated, "imprisonment for ninety days is not, in the abstract, a punishment which is either cruel or unusual. But the question cannot be considered in the abstract. Even one day in prison would be cruel and unusual punishment for the 'crime' of having a common cold."

The Supreme Court had spoken and a milestone had been

reached. Father Egan looked to the future with renewed optimism.

He had no way of knowing just how much that optimism was soon to be justified.

12. THE HAVEN

A CALL came to a New York newspaper shortly after the Court's decision. It was answered by a reporter who happened to be the present writer. For the past few days I had been checking into the incidence of addiction in the city. The caller introduced himself as Father Egan, a Graymoor priest in Greenwich Village. He said he had learned of my inquiries and thought he could be of some help. When I asked him how, he replied he was chaplain to Narcotics Anonymous.

"They call me the Junkie Priest," he added.

The newsroom was in its customary uproar. People were bellowing and the telephones were ringing constantly. I therefore thought I had not heard him correctly.

"They call you the *what?*" I asked.

Father Egan repeated it, and I grabbed my hat and ran to meet him.

From the conversation came a meeting with this obscure priest, a story on him in my newspaper and a subsequent article in *The Catholic Digest* which appeared in September, 1962, and briefly described his work. After the article was published Father Egan received the first of a series of cash gifts from throughout the world, one contribution coming from a Protestant congregation in Hawaii.

These first donations, totaling thirty-seven dollars, created a problem. Father Egan explained to his superior that the money was sent to him specifically for the purpose of helping his girls. He was quickly granted permission to put it aside and use it as he saw fit.

He counted the thirty-seven dollars again. Now that he had some money he decided to open a bank account. A bank was conveniently close to the House of Detention and he presented himself there one bright fall morning. He was, however, unsure as to how a bank account was opened for he had never made a deposit in his life. His studies of theology, he recalled, had not included anything on putting money in banks. But he walked into the air-conditioned atmosphere of the West Side Savings Bank, south of Eighth Street on Sixth Avenue, and was directed to an officer seated at a desk. Father Egan introduced himself and was astonished when the man stood up and vigorously pumped his hand.

"Glad to meet you, Father,' he said enthusiastically. "I read the article about you."

Father Egan pondered his new-found fame for a moment, then produced his thirty-seven dollars. He explained its purpose and said he wished to open an account with it. "And I hope to God it grows," he said.

Father Egan was speedily enrolled as one of the bank's depositors. When he left, the bank official drew the magazine article on Father Egan from his desk and looked at it thoughtfully. Then he took an elevator to the mezzanine floor and entered the office of Edgar T. Hussey, president.

Hussey is a square-faced, ruddy-complexioned man with steel-gray hair and an affable manner. He is a graduate of Manhattan College and is active in such local projects as the Greenwich Village Fresh Air Fund, which each year sends neighborhood children to summer camps. He is fond of emphasizing that his bank is a "community" bank and he derives considerable enjoyment from the Village's uniquely small-town atmosphere, which enables him to shop and chat with acquaintances on the neighborhood's sidewalks.

He read the article in silence, then tossed it on his desk. "Maybe we can help this priest sometime," he said briefly. "Next time he comes in here tell him I want to see him."

He then turned to other matters. But a few days later, when Father Egan sat before him, he listened carefully to a recitation of problems faced by women in the prison across the street. When Father Egan concluded he nodded.

"Interesting," he said. "Let's stay in touch."

Father Egan shrugged imperceptibly. So many were interested and so many left it just at that. He thanked the banker and walked out into the Sixth Avenue sunshine. The House stood massively outlined against a flawless sky.

The following day he received two telephone calls. The first was from the official he had met when he first entered the bank. He invited Father Egan to deliver a luncheon address to the Greenwich Village Kiwanis.

"Tell them everything," he urged. "You know, about the girls leaving the prison and being drug addicts and all that. You might get a surprise."

Father Egan nodded skeptically. He had had his surprises, most of them bad. He had received promises and assurances of help many times and few of them had materialized. But he accepted the invitation on the grounds that it could possibly create a little local sympathy for his girls and could even result in some kind of donation. Winter was coming and the girls would need warm clothing. Twenty-five or thirty dollars would be useful.

The second call was from Hussey. "Have lunch with me," the bank president said. It sounded more like a command than an invitation, and Father Egan became a little flustered.

"It's Friday," he said lamely. "I've got to eat fish."

"Meet me anyway. I want to talk to you."

Father Egan replaced the receiver slowly and wonderingly. A bank president?

At noon, however, he was walking on Sixth Avenue with Hussey toward the Captain's Table, a restaurant facing the House. Father Egan motioned to the prison.

"Girls come out of there every day," he said quietly. "Sometimes they need decent clothes to find a job. I've got a few things, some dresses, skirts and blouses that I bought and were given to me. But I've got no place to put them except maybe in the trunk of a car I borrow once in a while. And the girls haven't got anywhere to try them on. I've got nowhere to meet them except right here in the streets. Everything's done in the streets and in hamburger joints."

He added, gloomily, that everything was going wrong and that nobody cared. Hussey replied by remarking that Father Egan appeared somewhat antisocial.

"And why shouldn't I be antisocial?" Father Egan answered, with some bitterness. "Society keeps them in jail for months. Society does its duty. Now they're out of jail. So what does society do now?"

Hussey nodded, but reasoned that *he* was society and that *he* cared. So might others, providing they knew of the problem. "Look," he said. "In just these few minutes you've spelled out something I never even thought about before."

During the lunch Father Egan told Hussey how girls would call him at all hours to say they had not eaten or slept, sometimes for days. They would ask him if there was somewhere, anywhere, they could rest for an hour. Was there any place where they could iron a dress? Anywhere they could just sit down and relax?

Hussey nodded. "Then your immediate problem," he said crisply, "is just that—a place."

"Any place. Just so it's ours."

"If your need is so simple why haven't you made it known before?"

"I've been talking about halfway houses for years." Father Egan grinned. "But I've never met a bank president before."

They left the restaurant and turned south on Sixth Avenue. Hussey stopped almost immediately in front of a three-story building with a bar on its street floor. The upper windows were dilapidated and curtainless and it was obvious that the second and third floors were unoccupied.

"We've got the mortgage on this building," the banker murmured thoughtfully. "Two nice young guys run the bar and they run it clean. Maybe they'll let us have some space upstairs reasonably. Let's take a look, anyway?"

"You mean now?" asked Father Egan.

"Why not?" demanded the banker.

He secured a key from the bartender and with Father Egan trudged up three flights of steep, narrow stairs between discolored walls. On the upper floors the building had a musty, unused odor. Hussey unlocked the door on the third floor.

Father Egan walked in and found a large L-shaped room under a sloping glass roof. Sunlight poured through the panes and slanted across the dusty air. There was a bathroom and kitchenette. The room was empty, except for a broken chair tilted in one littered corner. The floor was uncovered and the room looked like an abandoned artist's studio, typical of many vaguely Bohemian apartments in Greenwich Village.

Father Egan walked to the large, almost wall-to-wall window at the far end of the room; it looked out on the busy intersection of Sixth Avenue and Eighth Street and on the opposite sidewalk a flower stall provided a splash of bright colors. It was the heart of the Village and by turning his head only slightly to the right he could look directly at the barred windows of the House of Detention.

He breathed deeply and looked about him again. As he did so, the empty shabbiness of the room seemed to dissolve and he saw a warm and softly lit lounge with comfortable furniture, a television set, coffee on the kitchen stove and his girls, his battered, bedraggled streetwalkers, seated and rested and safe. The vision disappeared and he turned to see Hussey watching him narrowly.

"Ed," Father Egan said quietly. "This is terrific. Terrific. If you could get this for us, this would be it."

Hussey nodded gravely.

Father Egan had to hurry to the bus station on Eighth Avenue to catch an upstate-bound bus and preach at a country parish during the weekend. When he returned, on Monday morning, he telephoned Hussey. He was astonished by what the banker had to say.

"You got the place," Hussey told him matter-of-factly. "And no rent for three months."

Father Egan sat down. It was unbelievable news. But his mind worked furiously.

"Ed, that's great," he said. "Just great. Can the girls sleep there? It's very important. Can they stay overnight?"

Hussey told him, emphatically, that they could not. The downstairs premises was a bar and a liquor license was involved. That precluded anyone remaining on the premises at night. But Father Egan was only mildly disappointed and he thanked and thanked his friend, hung up, and almost ran the two blocks from the Graymoor residence to the dusty apartment on Sixth Avenue.

He stood inside again, businesslike now, envisioning its

possibilities. At last he had a place. It wasn't quite a halfway house. But it was a *place*.

That day his mind rocketed with plans as he made his rounds at the prison, at Bellevue Hospital and on the streets. When he returned, at 4 P.M., he bounded up the stairs and was amazed once more.

The room was bustling with overalled plumbers, painters and plasterers. He beamed at them and prowled inside on an inspection. The most beautiful bathtub and shower he had ever seen had already been installed.

The following noon Father Egan and Ed Hussey arrived at the restaurant of the lower Fifth Avenue hotel where the priest was to make his speech to the Village Kiwanis. Hussey introduced Father Egan briefly and left.

Father Egan delivered his speech in his usual impassioned manner, telling the assembled business and professional men before him that the Village, as a community, had a responsibility to the unfortunate women released from the prison in its midst. He added, almost offhandedly, that when most women were freed they were without funds. Village stores, therefore, consequently suffered the heaviest from their shoplifting activities. Solemn head nodding greeted this and Father Egan knew he had touched a tender spot. He paused, timing himself carefully.

"But if it becomes known that you people are helping them," he declared, "I can get them to stop stealing in the Village. They'll only steal in other neighborhoods, where the people are less kind to them."

There was a moment's astonished silence, then a roar of laughter. When it subsided a member of the audience rose to ask Father Egan what he considered his most immediate, pressing requirement. Father Egan replied that this was in the process of being met and briefly described how he had acquired the third-floor apartment on Sixth Avenue.

"Well in that case," said the questioner, "we can adopt the place, can't we?"

Father Egan nodded, though not sure what was meant.

"I can send up a refrigerator and a washer and dryer," he heard someone say.

"And I'll give all the lamps, tables and chairs he needs," said another voice.

One man walked forward and handed Father Egan a check. It was for five hundred dollars. Father Egan stared at him in bewilderment.

A restaurant owner stood up. He was the proprietor of an old and famous Village establishment and he told Father Egan to send twelve girls each week for free meals.

"They're welcome as long as I'm alive," he said, and sat down.

Another restaurant owner rose from his chair. He urged Father Egan to send as many girls as wished to come to his restaurant, where they could eat without charge.

"They can eat five-dollar meals, ten-dollar meals, anything," he said. "Only just ask 'em not to come in the lunch and dinner rush hours."

A dentist called out that any of Father Egan's girls were welcome at his surgery, any time. First-class dental care, he said, would be on the house.

They passed a hat and handed it to Father Egan, sitting motionless among them. He counted its contents and shook his head slowly. The hat contained eight hundred dollars. Things were happening too quickly, he felt. After so many years of fighting alone it was not easy to realize that he had so many allies. He stood up amid cheers and laughter and the men crowded about him, shaking his hand.

For once his gift of oratory deserted him. He stammered that the donations were not for him, that he promised to use them only for his girls, to help them stay out of jail, to keep them from crime and degradation, to help them get a fresh start in life. . . .

That night in his room Father Egan pondered his new situation. He was silghtly confused by the speed of events and realized that as a priest he had certainly spent his years distant from the world of business and the methods by which some material problems could be solved. He also realized he had started an important community project with unforeseeable possibilities. It was no small undertaking and he wondered if he would be granted permission to devote time to it.

After all, he was technically the Junkie Priest only in his spare time. . . .

There was one way to find out. He dialed his superior.

The reply was as he expected. Father Egan was carefully but bluntly reminded that there was no permanence to his assignment in New York. He was subject to transfer to any Graymoor mission in the nation or the world at any time. He could not, therefore, assume any legal or financial responsibilities for the project. But he could, of course, aid any appropriate group or organization to operate it, provided they were prepared to incorporate it or be otherwise accountable.

He called Ed Hussey.

A few days later a meeting was convened in the thickly carpeted boardroom of the West Side Savings Bank. Around the long, polished table sat numerous prominent Villagers, including the captain of the local police precinct. Their topic of discussion was the legal process by which Father Egan's project could be launched.

Having placed these matters in safe hands, Father Egan next decided the apartment needed a name. He casually informed his girls in the House of the impending event and the news flashed through the cells: *Father Egan's opening a place for us girls*. He asked the girls to provide the name and a loosely organized contest subsequently developed inside the prison. They argued furiously and bombarded him with ideas. They suggested the Village Halfway House, the Village Shelter, the Village Home, but none seemed to strike the particular note he was seeking. At the bank he and Ed Hussey huddled over a thesaurus in search of more ideas. They thumbed to the word *shelter* and found *refuge, place of security, haven, sanctuary, retreat, sanctum, dugout, storm cellar, asylum, safety zone*. . . .

But it was only among a chorus of shouted suggestions in a jail corridor that the full name finally came to him:

THE VILLAGE HAVEN

That's it, he decided. It was perfect. Incorporation papers subsequently filed with the State of New York stated that:

We, the undersigned, for the purpose of forming a corporation pursuant to the membership corporation law of the State of New York, hereby certify:

First: the name of the corporation shall be the Village Haven, Inc.

Second: the purposes for which it is to be formed are as follows:

To give aid, comfort and relief to females discharged from penitentiaries, prisons, reformatories, jails, Houses of Detention and other correctional institutions in the State of New York by providing a place where such persons can obtain food, clothing, counseling and employment information to enable them to earn their own livelihood and maintain their place in the community as responsible citizens.

Father Egan read the document with great care and excitement. On it appeared the names of fifteen business and professional men and women, plus clergymen of the Protestant and Jewish faiths. It was an aseptic, dryly worded legal paper but he saw in it some of the most beautiful and moving prose ever written. *To give aid, comfort and relief . . .* The implications leaped at him from between the precisely typed lines.

But now—would the girls come to this haven?

A wind whipped briskly on Sixth Avenue as Father Egan and Ed Hussey stepped out of the Haven's street entrance. The cold was bitter for fall, forcing them to quicken their stride. In the room above, the floor was cluttered with a jumble of unwrapped appliances, unassembled furniture and cases of coffee cups and dishes. They had carried out a routine inspection for a few minutes until Father Egan had had to leave for his morning visit to the House of Detention. Hussey offered to accompany him across the street before returning to the bank. They dodged the traffic and approached the prison's entrance on Greenwich Avenue.

A dark-eyed girl with uncombed hair walked toward them. She wore a stained, shapeless coat and above her high-heeled shoes her bare legs were faintly blue with cold. She nodded to Father Egan, though he had not met her before.

He smiled at her and greeted her with his customary "Hi."

"You Father Egan?" she asked.

"That's me."

An addict, he judged expertly, though not using drugs now.

"Is your place ready yet, Father?" she asked directly.

Father Egan and Ed Hussey exchanged glances.

"No," Father Egan said quietly. "Not yet."

"Well," the girl persisted, "one of the officers in the House told me I could maybe go over there and take a bath. She said the bathroom was ready."

Father Egan raised his eyebrows. "Is that so?" he said. "And what does *she* know about it?"

"Everything goin' on up there is all over the jail," the girl replied. "We know what color it's been painted and everything."

Father Egan grinned and asked the girl when she had been released.

"Friday. I been waiting for you."

"This is Monday. Where've you been all weekend?"

"Sleeping here and there, you know. I sure could use a bath."

Father Egan and the banker looked at each other again.

"The hot water *is* running," Father Egan said hesitantly.

"It's cold up there," said Hussey. "No heat."

But Father Egan had made up his mind. He handed the girl the key to the Haven.

"Okay," he said. "Go take your bath."

"Wait," said Hussey. "Meet me in front of the place in five minutes. I've got an idea. I'm going to the bank. I'll be right back."

He hurried away and Father Egan and the girl walked across Sixth Avenue and waited in the hallway at the foot of the stairs leading to the Haven. Through the bar's glass doors the bartender eyed them curiously. In less than five minutes Hussey reappeared. He carried a large electric heater in each hand.

"I brought these from the bank," he puffed. "She can't take a bath without heat."

Upstairs they pushed furniture and packing cases aside and connected the heaters to newly installed outlets, fitted free of charge by a local contractor. They waited until the heaters cast a pleasant glow, then bade the girl an uncertain farewell.

When they returned, an hour later, they were astonished at the result. The Haven was cozily warm and the girl was barely recognizable. She had combed her hair, her skin glowed and she greeted them cheerfully. Would they, she asked, like some coffee? Following her bath she had shopped for coffee, milk and sugar and it was all ready. Father Egan and the bank president sat down. The girl poured daintily and they drank from the steaming cups.

"My name is Juanita," she volunteered. "Oh, this is such a nice place."

And Juanita was the Village Haven's first customer.

Father Egan received additional assistance, in an unexpected manner and from an unknown source. He received a telephone call from a stranger who said he was a Philadelphia automobile dealer in New York on a brief visit.

"I read about you," he said. "I want to give you a car."

Father Egan sighed. He politely told the caller to write him and that he would be glad to discuss the matter. Right now he was busy and—

"No, I'm not a nut," interrupted the caller. "Meet me in my room in the Waldorf Astoria in an hour."

Father Egan consequently was soon the surprised owner of a shiny, barely used Volkswagen station wagon. At the dealer's showroom he had been asked what color he wanted.

"Black."

"They don't come in black."

"Well paint it black. Then the cops will know it's mine and I won't get tickets."

The vehicle was painted black. In future months it became indispensable—and unmistakably his—as he carried clothes, food, baby carriages and furniture throughout the city. He drove the compact vehicle with relaxed and seemingly careless speed, dashing past other cars with barely inches to spare. He believed in making as many green lights as possible on a given street and derived glee out of startling jaywalking pedestrians with furious horn tooting.

He was utterly bewildered when a Village apartment-house owner granted him the rarest of New York City privileges— a private parking place in a basement garage, free.

In a month the room over the bar on Sixth Avenue was completely transformed. New York's strangest club had come into being.

In appearance it was virtually identical to the sudden vision experienced by Father Egan on the first day he had stepped inside the room. A green rug lay on the floor, matching the freshly painted walks. There were deep, comfortable couches, a dining table and chairs, a picture of Christ on one wall and a rabbi on another. The windows were bordered by flowered curtains. A new television set, gift of a well-known Village political figure, neatly filled one corner. In an alcove stood Father Egan's desk, already equipped with a telephone. At one end of the apartment a clothes rack stretched from wall to wall; it was heavy with an assortment of dresses and coats. A bookshelf was piled with women's blouses, underwear, belts, hats, purses and shoes. The kitchen gleamed with new appliances.

On one window ledge were perched a large number of brightly dressed children's dolls, though children were rarely if ever seen at the Haven. The dolls were hugged and fondled by women who had spent years in prisons, without normal family life or motherhood.

Father Egan's desk, plus an end table and one sofa, had come from the mortgage department of the West Side Savings Bank. Some chairs had been sent up from a restaurant on the same block. Other items in the room had poured in from Greenwich Village storekeepers. The Haven's curtains, though, had a story of their own.

Their fabric had come, routinely enough, as a gift from yet another Village store. On its arrival two former House inmates took measurements of the Haven's windows; Father Egan then took the measurements and fabric to the prisoners' workshop at the House of Detention. There, more measurements and other details were requested and he crossed once more to the Haven, secured the answers and returned to the prison. Before the curtains were completed and hung he had lost track of the number of times he made the journey back and forth between the Haven and the jail with questions and answers about how to hang curtains.

Gradually, as girls were released from the House they began to trickle into the Haven. None of them knew what to expect and some were cynical and suspicious as well as curious. Many were drawn, however, by a leaflet written by Father Egan, mimeographed in the prison and circulated through its twelve unyielding floors:

AFTER I LEAVE . . .

WHAT?

"Nobody REALLY cares what happens to me. . . ."
"Nobody gives a damn. . . ."
"If only I got a real break. . . ."
"I'd never come back to this place if I got help when I leave. . . ."

Over the years I've heard many girls say this. We've all heard about it. Maybe you've said it yourself.
Maybe you were sincere when you said it. Maybe you were not. "Promises" are bad to make in prison. Girls count on them. So this isn't a promise. It's only a maybe. Maybe we can help you.
So at least give us a try. Even if we can't help you in the exact way you want help, at the exact time you want it, at least we will be nice to you. To us you're not an ex-inmate or a girl with a record. You're a PERSON, a human being, a woman in need.

Directly across the street from the House, at 404 Sixth Avenue, next to Whelan's Drug Store, on the third floor above the Belmar Restaurant, you'll find

THE VILLAGE HAVEN

The girls in the House decided on its name, "The Haven." For those of you who use it, it is just what you called it . . . a Haven.

Maybe you can see it from your window, especially at nighttime. But to really appreciate it, you have to visit it. There's a kitchen with refrigerator and stove—to make yourself a meal. There's a new washer, dryer, iron and iron board—to do your clothes. There's even a dryer for your hair. There are facilities for a bath and shower.

And oh! What a beautiful living room with a TV, soft couches and a fireplace. And there's a phone . . . and clothing—if you need any . . . and maternity and baby clothing, too.

The Village Haven is open every day from 9 A.M. to 11 P.M. You're welcome during these hours so long as you're not drinking or on pills or junk. Neither are you welcome if you're coming to "con" us in any way.

But if you need any real EMERGENCY help, or if you just want to relax, eat, wash, get some necessary clothing, or seek advice about a job . . . or a place to live . . .

You're Welcome at the Village Haven.

The Greenwich Village Community has set up this "Haven" to help you get a start when you leave. It's one of the nicest things done for you by any community. The more you use The Village Haven, so much more will people see the need of helping you after you leave. . . .

Come visit us . . .
FR. EGAN

Consequently if a dozen girls were released from the House during a morning perhaps three of them would walk into the Haven. They frequently returned on following nights and the room was crowded on many evenings. Newcomers read the signs and instructions plastered all over the walls with fascination. No one had ever seen anything like it.

One sign urged:

LET'S NOT TALK ABOUT JUNK
OR THE HOUSE OF D.
LET'S TRY *SQUARE TALK*

Others said:

> IT ISN'T THE 7TH THAT HOOKS YOU
> IT'S THAT DAMN FIRST FIX THAT
> DOES IT.
>
> EASY DOES IT
> ONE DAY AT A TIME
>
> TODAY IS THE TOMORROW
> I WORRIED ABOUT YESTERDAY

Another read:

> IT WILL RUIN ALL THE GOOD WE
> HOPE TO DO IF YOU:

1. Drink alcohol on the way in or out.
2. Come here on drugs or with it on you.
3. Loiter or hang around outside in the hallway.
4. Bring men with you.
5. Wave across to girls in the House.

> THE POLICE WANT US TO SUCCEED
> DON'T *YOU* MAKE THEM CLOSE US UP

On one wall a girl painted a Disney-like mural showing a pathway receding into a gentle vista of mountains, trees and pastures. The path was lettered with the words:

> TAKE ONE STEP AT A TIME AND IF YOU SLIP DON'T STAY
> DOWN. . . . EVERY JOURNEY BEGINS WITH THE FIRST
> STEP. . . .

Shortly after the Haven opened, Greenwich Village housewives, Girl Scouts and social workers arrived to volunteer their help. At first there were some who were terrified at the thought of being alone with drug addicts, prostitutes and thieves. Soon, however, it became difficult to distinguish the volunteers from the ex-prisoners and it was not uncommon for a new girl to greet a volunteer with, "Hi, how long you been out?" So many women offered their services that a duty roster was established, assigning each woman to certain hours on certain days. It became customary at the Haven for at least one woman volunteer to be present at all times.

Initially the Haven was open from 11 A.M. to 1 P.M., then from 6:30 P.M. to 10:30 P.M. But Father Egan found a group of girls waiting outside the building one morning at 10 A.M., so he promptly opened up. Another shivering group formed at 9 A.M. and he pulled the opening time back once more. In addition he found he virtually had to drive girls out of the Haven at 1 P.M. He therefore decided to keep open all day, and the hours of 9 A.M. to 11 P.M. were eventually settled on.

He instituted a survey of the number of meals being served and it was discovered that over a two-week period more than two hundred breakfasts, lunches and dinners had been consumed. Curiously, the girls preferred to eat at the Haven than at the two excellent Village restaurants where, as Father Egan's charges, they were welcome to dine lavishly and free.

Food arrived mysteriously at the Haven. He would find dozens of cans stacked on kitchen shelves that had been depressingly bare the previous day. Some were brought in by women volunteers. Girl Scouts staggered up the three flights of stairs with weighty cartons of foodstuffs in their arms.

The Haven had virtually no formal rules except those posted on its walls and the girls were given unrestricted use of the kitchen. They cooked and ate whatever they wished, whenever they wished. Each evening, though, a substantial meal was prepared for everyone present. For Father Egan, this was the day's highlight, when the girls sat together at the table chattering and devouring platefuls of food.

During one dinner the door opened and a uniformed policeman entered the room. The girls froze and the Haven became silent. Father Egan stared levelly at the young patrolman. The uniform seemed alien and hostile in the casual room.

The officer looked around. He beamed.

("He had a big Irish, Jewish or Italian face," Father Egan remembered, "and it just lit up.")

"Well now," said the officer. "Now isn't this nice? I didn't know you had the place fixed up so pretty."

The girls eyed him stonily.

"I just came up to tell you," he continued, "that some of the fellers at the precinct have got you a new table and six chairs and we're gonna send 'em up. Anything else we can do, just let us know."

He smiled approvingly at everyone and left, closing the door softly. For a minute no one in the Haven moved.

Then Juanita said, "Well I'll be damned," and the tension broke.

But another evening the door was flung open violently, bringing the girls to their feet. A teen-ager burst into the room, sobbing hysterically.

"Oh, I ran an' I ran an' I ran," she cried. "Thank God you're open."

"What're you running from?" Father Egan demanded.

"I been runnin' from him for seven blocks," she panted. "If you hadn't been open he'd have caught me and beaten me up."

"Who would?"

"My husband."

Father Egan looked at the other girls and shrugged. The girls calmed the newcomer and made room for her at the table. Her explanation was baffling but, like so much at the Haven, was accepted without question.

One night he discovered the Haven's front door key was missing. He obtained a duplicate but the missing key disturbed him. A few nights later the downstairs bartender approached him on the sidewalk. He had seen a light burning in the Haven's window long after closing time, he said. This was serious, for if anyone was staying at the Haven overnight he was in danger of losing his tavern license. He warned that the Haven might have to close. Father Egan promised to investigate.

That evening he ostentatiously tacked a new sign on the Haven's wall. It asked whoever had taken the key to return it at once and no more would be said. He sat at his desk and waited as the girls crowded about the sign.

Within a few minutes a stout girl with a cast in one eye

and pockmarked skin walked to the table and placed the key before him. She began to cry and admitted she had been sleeping at the Haven after everyone had left for the night.

"I don't feel *safe* no place else, Father," she wailed. "There's all kinds of mean guys roamin' around this town. I didn't mean no harm. I just lay down on the couch and went to sleep."

He sighed and calmed her. He felt as if he were spending a great deal of his life, calming tearful, frightened women and he hoped again that some day there would indeed be somewhere in New York where his girls could spend their nights feeling safe. Just a few nights before, Juanita had wistfully remarked that it was a pity that everyone had to separate at closing time.

"We have nice evenings together here"—she shrugged— "then when we close up we all go someplace different, to this hotel, that hotel, this dump, that dump. Wouldn't it be better if we could all stay in one place and have breakfast together in the morning?"

But he had little time to reflect on Juanita's words, for a girl named Yvonne entered the room and waved cheerfully at him. At seventeen Yvonne was tall and attractive and her wide features bore the prominent cheekbones and tilted eyes of her Indian birth in Wisconsin. She had run away from home at the age of twelve and had been, as far as he knew, in and out of reformatories and prisons since. She was, however, fond of claiming that her father was a chief and her brothers were princes.

She walked up to his desk and spread one hundred dollars in ten-dollar bills before him.

"I brought you a present, Father," she said. "For the Haven."

Father Egan looked at the money, eyed the girl quizzically, then tilted his chair back.

"Where'd you get it, Princess?" he asked wearily.

Yvonne shrugged and smiled.

Father Egan leaned forward, gathered the bills in one hand and threw them on the floor at Yvonne's feet.

"Dirty money, Yvonne," he said calmly. "Get it out of here."

The smile died from Yvonne's face. She scooped up the money and walked quickly from the room. The others watched her departure in silence.

Some weeks later Yvonne telephoned him—collect—from Houston.

"I want to come home, Father," she said. "I'm broke and I'm pregnant. I've been working in a bar and I've been arrested four times. Please send me bus fare."

He did.

Once a newcomer to the Haven used an obscenity in Father Egan's presence. She was immediately engulfed in a welter of flying fists, shoes and purses, hurled bodily to a couch and pummeled mercilessly until two volunteer workers flung themselves on the heap of screaming, furious girls and forcibly separated them. The shaken victim was then informed, with unmistakable underworld menace, that if she ever used similar language in Father Egan's presence again she would be in *real* trouble.

As 1962 neared its end a shimmering, glittering Christmas tree illuminated the Haven's window. In the House, women remained awake far into the night to gaze at the tree, which could be clearly seen from between their bars. When Christmas passed and the tree was removed some prisoners were heard to remark glumly that the dousing of the tree's lights simply meant that another year of empty prison life was about to begin.

This was duly relayed to Father Egan. He explained the problem to a friend, who happened to own an electrical appliance store. That night a multicolored lantern shone brightly in the Haven's window. To the women in the House, to others on the streets, to girls emerging from subway exits, the lantern assumed an identity and meaning of its own. When it was lit, it was the sign that the Haven was open and that there was somewhere in the city where they were welcome.

The Haven's three-month rent-free period had now expired. Money became an even more pressing problem than usual—the rent was $150 per month. Money was also needed for clothing, food, medical supplies and hotel rooms. Somehow, the problems were solved. A neighborhood Jewish delicatessen sent up a huge baked Virginia ham. Through the Village Lions' Club an optometrist pledged to provide the girls with free glasses.

These financial troubles also came to the attention of the Progressive Era Association, a Village organization with membership composed of Italian and Italian-descent local residents. Without hesitation, a collection was taken for Father Egan and he was presented with several hundred dollars' worth of checks.

Later, when he reached the bank, he discovered that each check had been made out not to "Father Daniel Egan," as his account was listed, but to "The Junkie Priest." This precipitated some minor and jovial confusion at the bank and finally he was asked to endorse each check: "Father Egan, Junkie Priest."

He was indeed now known better as the Junkie Priest than by his own name. His hurrying figure and black station wagon had become familiar sights on the Village streets. Yet there were few who were aware of how even a routine day was spent in the Junkie Priest's extraordinary life.

13. A DAY IN NEW YORK

IT IS 6:45 A.M. on a spring day in New York. The streets are rustling with early movement as the sun climbs over the vast, restless city. The air is cool, but mist shrouds the spires of midtown skyscrapers, bringing promise of warmth and blue skies.

In the small chapel of the Graymoor residence in Greenwich Village, Father Egan is offering daily Mass. He prays for God's help during this new day and whispers, "Dear God, junkies aren't *really* junkies, they're Your children, all of them. Whatever I do to help them, by Your divine assistance, I do for You. If I had any other motives I'd have quit it all years ago. . . ."

An hour later, after breakfast, he telephoned three sleepy girls in three cheap hotel rooms. For each his message was the same.

"Get up," he ordered. "Eight o'clock. Time to go to work. Don't be late or you'll lose the job. Call me this evening. Don't even *think* about junk today. God bless you."

By 8:15 he was on the other side of Manhattan, now rumbling with heavy morning traffic. In the emergency room at Bellevue he met Lola, as arranged the previous evening. Lola, a slow-moving Negro girl, nine months pregnant, was waiting patiently.

Father Egan took an intern to one side.

"She's in danger of losing the kid," he confided. "Or maybe the baby will be born addicted. With her, anything can happen. She's been a drug addict a long time. Better find her a bed."

Lola was admitted.

On another floor, in the somber confines of Bellevue's barred prison ward, he stopped for a moment by Janie's bed. The girl, a thin, freckle-faced redhead with a pinched, wrinkled face, had recovered from a gruesome arm infection caused by repeated heroin injections with a blunt, unwashed needle. Today she was to be discharged from the hospital and was scheduled to be returned to Women's Court for sentencing. One month earlier she had pleaded guilty to a charge of prostitution, for perhaps the fortieth time.

"Hi, Janie." He grinned. "So how's the arm?"

"Father, you came to see me." Janie was pleased. "The arm's okay, but how much time is the judge gonna give me?"

He scribbled a note on a pad, ripped it off and handed it to her.

"Make sure this gets to the judge," he said. "It's a plea for a suspended sentence."

The note asked the judge to take into account the time Janie had spent in the prison ward. It promised he would immediately arrange for her to be sent to Lexington and that the Village Haven would try to find her a job and a place to live when she returned.

By 9 A.M. Father Egan was driving downtown on Second Avenue, whistling cheerfully. At Seventeenth Street he parked the Volkswagen and cast a shrewd eye at the side entrance to Manhattan General Hospital. Four men and three women walked out; the men immediately hailed a cab on Second Avenue. Father Egan watched as the women dug into their purses. They were pooling funds to buy drugs. He got out of the station wagon and walked toward them. They eyed him guardedly.

"Don't do it," he said, shaking his head. "You just got out of hospital. What's the sense? Forget about it for today, huh?"

He reasoned and argued and pleaded for a few minutes, then stopped abruptly as two women suddenly detached themselves, walked quickly to Second Avenue and stopped a passing taxi. The other accompanied him to the station wagon. One out of three, he thought. Not bad. He drove her to the Village Haven, where a volunteer worker served her breakfast.

It was now 9:30 and the day had begun to fall into its familiar, relentless pattern. On his desk there were fresh messages. He leafed through them until one caught his eye: it was from the medical office at the House of Detention. Someone had been trying to reach him since 9 A.M., when Brenda, a girl discharged from the prison three days before, had called from a West Ninety-Fourth Street hotel room. He dialed the medical office and reached a prison doctor who told him the girl had been incoherent, sobbing and begging to be allowed to return to the jail. This was not unusual, but his cheerfulness vanished and his face settled into the lines that were to mark it for the rest of the day.

"She was crying that she was alone, pregnant, on dope, with no rent, no friends, no family, no nothing," the doctor was saying. "Apart from that she's in great shape. I think *somebody* ought to go see her."

Father Egan rammed his station wagon through the traffic-jammed Manhattan streets, driving as if it were a police car with siren screaming. He ignored outraged cries from taxi drivers and pedestrians, some of whom were startled to see the white collar around his neck. He drove uptown on Sixth Avenue, swerved left on Twenty-Third Street, reached the West Side Highway and sped north to the fringe of Harlem.

The station wagon halted in a no-parking zone on the dingy block. It was a tough neighborhood. Local residents, seated on front steps, watched impassively as the priest emerged and hurried into the hotel entrance. At his brusque request the clerk admitted him to Brenda's room.

She burst into fresh tears when she saw him. Father Egan relaxed and telephoned the doctor at the House of Detention.

"She's okay, now, Doc. I've got her. Phone Bellevue and arrange for a voluntary admission, will you? Yeah, she'll come with me. . . ."

So far all was routine.

Thirty minutes later he was back in Greenwich Village, parked outside the Haven. There he could watch as prisoners were released from the House. After a short wait he counted eleven women emerging into the Greenwich Avenue sunlight. They crossed Sixth Avenue at the Ninth Street intersection, some turning to shout and laugh at former cellmates waving frantically from cell windows. Several passers-by stared at the ex-prisoners with undisguised disgust and contempt. Four women entered a bar. When they came out one was carrying a bottle. They stopped a taxi and headed uptown. Four others hailed a taxi and also disappeared in an uptown direction.

The three remaining women halted beside the station wagon and peered in questioningly. There was only one such vehicle in the Village and they had spotted it as soon as they walked out of the House.

He jerked his thumb at the Haven's entrance. "Go on up," he said. "Coffee's ready. Use the phone. Relax." He followed them, and the stairs seemed longer and steeper than earlier in the day.

With the new arrivals, seven girls were in the Haven. One was stretched full-length on a couch, asleep. A needle-scarred arm lay across her face. Father Egan peered at her briefly. She had a mannish haircut and features and wore a man's shirt and close-fitting black slacks. He shook his head and sat down.

"Who's for lunch at a good restaurant and then a movie tonight?" he asked. The girls nodded quietly. He wrote notes of introduction to the two restaurants and the nearby movie theater catering to his girls without charge. The owners didn't realize what their generosity meant, he thought. It wasn't just food and entertainment. During a meal and a movie the girls would not even think about drugs, and that was a success in itself, if only for a few hours.

He made each girl promise she would return to the Haven after lunch and assured them that hotel rooms would be found that evening, that the city's Welfare Department would be contacted and that he would try to find them jobs.

Twelve noon.

A call from the city's probation office. "You know Mona, don't you, Father? Yeah, the blonde. Well, the judge says he'll turn her loose if she'll go back to Lexington for another try. Can you get her in there?"

Without her knowledge, a series of rapid telephone conversations ensued concerning Mona, a depressed girl sitting in a prisoners' waiting room in the Criminal Courts Building in downtown Manhattan. Father Egan's first call was to the Federal Narcotics Bureau in Washington, D.C. He reached a top bureau official and informed him he needed a bed in Lexington in a hurry. He gave the girl's name and briefly outlined her background; he knew it by memory. Five convictions for prostitution, two for theft, two for possession of drugs, innumerable arrests. One previous "cure" at Lexington. The official promised to call back in ten minutes, and did. A bed would be ready for Mona on Monday. Father Egan thanked him and promised he would see Mona arrived on time. He dialed the probation office.

"All set," he announced. "Lexington on Monday."

The probation officer called back within minutes. Everything was arranged. The judge had suspended Mona's sentence for a prostitution conviction and was sending her to the Haven in the morning, care of Father Egan. Father Egan nodded and made still one more call—to the Welfare Department's Division of Transportation. Could Mona's bus fare to Lexington be paid? It could. The rest was up to Mona.

One of the girls just released from the jail handed him a cup of coffee. He swallowed it and hurried out. He was behind schedule.

Twelve-thirty. The hospital ward at the House of Detention.

Father Egan walked from bedside to bedside. Seven addicts watched him apathetically. He spoke to each, promising to telephone Donna's mother and Laura's husband, get Patricia's clothing from the cleaners, find a lawyer for Carmen, bring cigarettes for Gertrude, maternity clothing for Teresa, find a hotel room for Rita.

"It may be good to be sick," he told them. "You know, like a blessing in disguise. It gives you a chance to think things over. It can force you to admit you've had it, that you're tired. Any time you feel like taking a fix, just remember the way you feel now."

At 1 P.M. Father Egan was on the jail's ground floor, reading messages left for him in his envelope-mailbox. All were from inmates due for release and seeking help outside. He gave their names to a guard, and while waiting for them to be sent down to him, drank a glass of milk in the second-floor kitchen.

They stepped off the elevator and sat on a corridor bench, dressed in blue and green prison dresses. He listened carefully to each girl; it was like hearing a phonograph record with the needle jammed hopelessly in one groove: *Father, I don't want to hustle any more. I don't want to use drugs again. I don't want to come back here.*

Sick at heart, he walked out of the jail. The time was 2:30.

He crossed Sixth Avenue again. How many times, he wondered, did he walk across this intersection during a single week? In the Haven, Manuela looked up from her sewing machine and smiled.

Weeks ago, sweating in the effort to stay away from heroin, she had told him she liked to sew. So he had toured Third Avenue's pawnshops one rainy morning and returned with an old but workable machine. It had been worth the time, money and effort to see the expression on Manuela's olive-skinned face. She had gasped with pleasure and stroked the machine with maternal care. Now she sat by it day after day, evening after evening. Once, when someone had brought her a dress to be altered and paid ten dollars for the work, she had fled from the Haven and returned with a carton of groceries. She spent the first money she had ever earned on the Haven. And

she informed Father Egan, to his indescribable satisfaction:
"Sewing is my new drug, Father."

More telephone messages waited for him. One—simply,
Jean called—made him uneasy.

He knew Jean. Aged twenty-five, she was a sad-faced
Bronx girl with an alarming heroin habit. How so slim a
frame could absorb such repeated, enormous doses of the
powerful drug was beyond him. But somehow, year after
year, Jean survived. Occasionally he would meet her, either
in the House, or in Bellevue, or on the street. Once she had
been a talented dancer and singer, but her former lustrous
beauty had long vanished. She had been disowned by her
family for years, except for a brother who regularly and
patiently appeared in courtrooms, always with enough bail
money.

She had once mused dreamily, "Father, I don't know why I
do it. I don't even enjoy it. But, somehow, I just got to. . . ."

He leafed through his notebook, found Jean's number and
dialed it. There was no answer. He hung up and dialed
again. No answer. He replaced the receiver slowly. She could
be out, she could be anywhere. But she had never telephoned
him before. Something was wrong. There was no time to lose.

Suddenly he was running from the room, startling his girls,
and leaping down the Haven's staircase. He slid behind the
wheel of the station wagon and shot the vehicle into the
Sixth Avenue traffic.

If he had driven fast during the morning he now disre-
garded all caution. He slammed the vehicle in and out of
snarled street congestion and thrust his foot down hard as
he hit the ramp leading to the West Side Highway.

Fifteen minutes after leaving the Haven, he swerved to a
halt in front of a crumbling hotel in the West Seventies, a
dank structure occupied almost exclusively by tenants living
on public welfare plus prostitutes and drug addicts.

"Get the keys to 4B and come with me," he snapped at the
desk clerk. Something in Father Egan's voice made the clerk
obey. Wordlessly they rode a whining elevator to the fourth
floor. Father Egan rapped on the door of the fifteen-dollar-
a-week room. He waited exactly five seconds, then instructed
the clerk to open up.

Jean was sprawled on the floor, her dyed blonde hair in disarray. She was clothed. Her breathing was labored, coming in short, hoarse gasps.

"Call police and an ambulance," Father Egan ordered the clerk.

He knelt by her side and prayed. *Please God, don't let her die. She's not ready to face You.*

A siren wailed on the street and when two uniformed patrolmen walked into the room he slowly rose to his feet.

"What seems to be the trouble?" demanded one of the officers.

Father Egan looked at him with distaste. They always asked the same question. Wasn't it obvious what the trouble was? All he had to do was look on the floor.

"Her name's Jean Herman," he said flatly. "She's twenty-five. She lives here. Her family lives in the Bronx; her father owns a dress factory. She's a drug addict. She's taken a serious overdose of heroin. She's unconscious. Now, the ambulance hasn't arrived, so will you please get her to a hospital at once?"

The two patrolmen ignored the request and peered at the girl on the floor.

"A drug addict, huh?" mused one. He took a black notebook from his pocket and scratched in it laboriously. Father Egan's irritation increased.

The officer searched through a bureau drawer, looked into a closet and lifted the mattress from the bed. The other patrolman raised the girl's lifeless right arm, observed the needle marks and nodded knowingly.

"Needle marks," he said.

Father Egan glared at him. "You don't say?" Bitterly, he lashed at the two officers. "You're not interested in helping this girl," he said. "You're just looking for an excuse to arrest her. What are you, promotion hungry? Look at you, you're searching the place, looking for junk and a needle. You want to put her in jail and she never hurt anyone in her life. She's sick, and all you can think of is finding something to rap her with. . . ."

The two patrolmen endured it stoically.

The ambulance arrived and he followed the howling vehicle on its journey downtown. Jean was very ill, he was told, and had taken an overdose so massive that it would have easily killed a non-user of drugs. But she would live.

"Thanks, Doc. I'll stop by tomorrow. Let me know if she needs anything."

He drove to a church on West Seventy-First Street, and in its dim interior his nerves, strung taut by the uncertainty over Jean, slowly relaxed. He prayed, wishing fervently that his addicts were with him to absorb the presence of God. He fought an overpowering desire to sleep by remaining on his knees for forty-five minutes.

Later, his morale rose as he entered the Haven. He was confronted with a pleasant sight and experienced a sensation akin to triumph. Two girls were cooking supper, Manuela was sewing, another was fixing her hair, others were watching television.

And all would have been working the streets without the Haven. They were clean addicts, off junk. Here was Kay, in the kitchen, clean now for a month. Clare hadn't touched a needle in six months. Louise was gaining weight after a two-week abstinence. Maybe they were cured, maybe they weren't. But while at the Haven they had a chance.

When he sat down he realized the extent of his fatigue. He telephoned the hospital. Jean was recovering rapidly.

Two new girls walked in and were served supper, no questions asked. Later they told him they had been released from Lexington three days before and had immediately returned to drugs and prostitution. Now they had no money for rent and had not eaten for thirty-six hours.

"We're at the end of our rope, Father," one girl said and shrugged. "We just ain't gettin' anywhere."

He began dialing his list of hotels. The fourth call resulted in a double room for twenty-four dollars a week. He took a chance and handed the two strangers twenty-four dollars and a note to the desk clerk.

"Just see you use it for room rent and nothing else," he said.

Eight P.M.

A neatly stacked pile of letters lay on his desk. His pencils were sharpened. The desk drawers were neat and ordered.

His appointment calendar was up to date. This was the work of Marguerite, a tall Negro girl who supervised his paper work with tyrannical thoroughness. Every evening she examined each item on the desk with the efficiency of a veteran secretary, though no office had ever employed her. Marguerite excelled at any secretarial task, but was unable to find work. She had spent seven years in prisons, on narcotics, prostitution and theft charges. They were years difficult to account for on application forms.

This evening there were the usual letters from the Women's Federal Prison at Alderson, West Virginia, and from the women's wards at Lexington. He was about to write brief replies when the door swung open and a girl entered, her white blouse reddened with blood. The girls crowded around her. He pushed his way through and eyed the newcomer carefully. She was in her teens, with shoulder-length blonde hair and chalk-white features. She wore dark glasses.

"I just fell asleep in a cellar and a guy tried to grab me and I hit him and he cut me," she said reasonably, as if this were a normal and not unusual sequence of events. Father Egan examined the blood-encrusted knife slash etched horizontally below her throat.

"Two inches higher and . . ."

He stopped and looked at her meaningfully. Did she know who had slashed her? No, she had never met him before. Why was she sleeping in a cellar? She was tired. He took her hand and drove her to nearby St. Vincent's Hospital.

When he climbed back up the stairs he heard raised voices in the room above. A girl had walked in, drowsy with heroin, and a "clean" addict had pointed sternly to the sign on the door stating:

YOU'RE WELCOME AT THE HAVEN
SO LONG AS YOU'RE OFF DRUGS

"So beat it," the clean addict was saying to the junkie.

"So I just came to say hello," was the answer.

"So hello and good-bye."

"Break it up," he interrupted. He took the girl to his desk and filled out an application form for admission to Manhattan General Hospital. Would she agree to go there? She shrugged, smiled and nodded. He wasn't sure whether it was a junkie's nod or an expression of agreement, but he made her promise to be at the hospital at 9 A.M. If she had come to the Haven, he reasoned, it was at least an indication that she wanted to be cured.

There were reasons for not permitting active, drug-taking addicts to remain in the Haven. It could develop into a shooting gallery, overrun with junk, and would not be open long. More than that, though, abstaining addicts became dangerously and often disastrously uneasy in the presence of users. A recent television program had dramatically demonstrated this.

The show had attempted to compare addiction control methods in England, where some addicts could obtain narcotics on a doctor's prescription, with methods in the United States, where most addictive drugs were contraband. The screen had shown detailed motion pictures, taken in England, of a young male addict injecting himself with legally acquired heroin. While watching, many girls in the Haven had become highly nervous; heroin had dominated their lives for years and was still perilously close to the surface of their thoughts. He regretted permitting the television show to be seen, but disliked telling the girls what and what not to do.

The British system, he considered, would create chaos if attempted in the United States. There were fewer addicts in all Britain at any given moment than there were in the House of Detention any night. If so-called narcotic clinics were opened in New York, thousands of police would be needed to control the crowds. The junkies would be lining up for blocks. Britain had a more cohesive, stable population and many conditions there did not parallel those in the United States. In Britain the police did not carry guns. Here, at least in some sections of the city, it could be a grim joke, even suicidal, for police to be unarmed.

Eight-thirty.

He remembered he hadn't eaten. He was about to do so when the telephone rang. A woman asked his help to get her daughter into Lexington. Sure, he said, send her over. A Newark, New Jersey, probation officer called. Could he bring a girl for Father Egan to talk to? Sure, bring her over. A girl

telephoned to tell him she needed a baby carriage. He hesitated, then promised to try to find one, and made a note to
stop at pawnshops in the morning. Another called to tell him
she had missed reporting to her probation officer.

"How many times?"

"Four. They got a warrant out for me. I'm in a jam. Can
you help me out?"

"Why didn't you report?"

"I don't know. Maybe I like trouble."

All right, he would try.

Nine-thirty.

A heavy-featured, unattractive girl entered the Haven, her
face puffy, her body swollen with pregnancy. She complained
of fever and said she was unable to eat. He drove her to
Bellevue.

It was close to 10 P.M. when he returned. The Haven's
lights were low and the room flickered with shadows as the
girls silently watched *Naked City* on television. He stayed
for a few moments, dropping subway tokens on his desk in
case anyone needed them. Then he left. He did not like to be
present when the Haven closed and the girls had to be sent
into the street. It was the moment when anything or everything that had been achieved by the Haven could be instantly shattered. The street was the jungle, and tigers lurked
in its gloom. It made no sense to lock the girls out at night,
when they were most in need of shelter and protection. He
walked slowly across Sixth Avenue, the House of Detention
a giant shadow to his right, and turned toward Waverly
Place.

He knelt in the Graymoor chapel to say his rosary.

The telephone rang. It was Bellevue.

"Better come on over," a nurse said. "There's a girl here
who doesn't look too good. She keeps asking for you."

"Who?"

"Dolores something-or-other."

"Yes, I know her. What happened?"

"She's been knifed."

He fled to the station wagon and again hurtled it across
the city, his lips moving in prayer.

He prayed for Dolores, a speck on the surface of the city's huge, turbulent sea. Sometime, somehow, Dolores had come from San Juan's shacks to the new life in the metropolis of the north and had become lost and abandoned in its endless, exitless labyrinth, another dark-skinned face on the swarming streets. For Dolores, life was nothing but the street and heroin to warm her scrawny frame. She was Negro, she was Puerto Rican, she spoke only the machine-gun-paced Spanish of her native island. She was nothing, she was nobody, she was a skinny, crafty-eyed junkie on a tenement's front step, a thieving, deadpan hustler on a Harlem sidewalk. She could not read, she could not write. Her skin hung loosely on her thin bones, she was twenty years old, she carried a razor-edged knife inside her dress and her price was three dollars.

He had met her in the House of Detention. Through an interpreter she had asked him to find out why she had not heard from her husband for several days. He had checked and learned her husband had died forty-eight hours earlier in Brooklyn's grim Raymond Street jail. He told her, with all the gentleness and care he could summon, and was faintly disturbed by the absence of emotion on the small, brooding face.

But a week later, while he was showing another priest through the House, Dolores had broken away from a corridor cleaning detail and run to him. She flung her arms about him, hugging him tightly. As he gently disengaged himself he smiled in embarrassment at his companion and said, "This doesn't happen very often."

The priest had not returned the smile. Instead he said quietly, "That was one of the most beautiful things I have ever seen."

Now Father Egan increased the station wagon's speed as it rushed through the night toward Bellevue.

In the emergency room he hurried to Dolores' bedside. She was unable to speak. She moved her lips wordlessly, her eyes enormous with pain. She had been stabbed seventeen times.

"Dolores," he whispered. "It's me. Father Egan."

The girl's face, dark against the whiteness of the pillow,

twitched slightly. She reached out and grasped Father Egan's hand, then died. He gave her absolution.

He wept unashamedly. Dolores, poor Dolores, now like one of the waxen dolls at the Haven. Tears streamed from his face as he begged God to be merciful to her.

"Her addiction was more compulsion than sin, O Lord. See not her sins, but remember Thy infinite mercy."

Doctors and nurses watched in silence as he walked wearily from the emergency room.

It was insane, he told himself. In an age of dazzling, exploding science why should anyone live and die this way? What was missing, what was absent? His own fight was so tiny and isolated a corner of the struggle against human suffering and, accordingly, so little was needed to win. He thought of Helen, the first addict he had known, in the East Side church so long ago, of Marie, still forlorn on the Upper West Side, of Lois, Corinne and Anita and Yvonne and all the others. Why should so cruel a fate befall them? And how many of them would have been granted their God-given rights to healthy bodies and minds if, during all these years, there had existed some manner of enlightened rehabilitation system? For if anyone needed to pause before entering the world again it was the female addict. No one had so many strikes against her, no one had less chance to live without pain and fear and shame. Here was New York, streets and streets, buildings and buildings, stretching for miles under the skies and stars, and there was little else that comforted them but a small room over a Sixth Avenue bar. Maybe one day, though, there would be something more. It would be a house, not an institution but a house, where they could rest after prison terms and addiction cures. It would be air-conditioned in summer and warm in winter and there would be fresh flowers and plenty of food and no bars in the windows.

Father Egan swung the station wagon into Sixth Avenue and drove past the House of Detention. To his left the Haven's window was dark. But it would be bright again the next day. And that, he reflected, was at least a beginning.